PAUL'S SHORT LETTERS BIBLE STUDY

PRACTICAL WISDOM FROM TEN LIFE-CHANGING EPISTLES

40-DAY BIBLE STUDY SERIES
BOOK 16

PETER DEHAAN

- Developmental editor: Julie Harbison
- Copyeditor: Robyn Mulder
- Cover design: Fanderclai Design
- Author photo: Chelsie Jensen Photography

To Nate Bull

Series by Peter DeHaan

40-Day Bible Study Series takes a fresh and practical look into Scripture, book by book.

Bible Character Sketches Series celebrates people in Scripture, from the well-known to the obscure.

Holiday Celebration Devotionals rejoice in the holidays with Jesus.

Visiting Churches Series takes an in-person look at church practices and traditions to inform and inspire today's followers of Jesus.

Be the first to hear about Peter's new books and receive updates at PeterDeHaan.com/updates.

CONTENTS

PAUL'S SHORT LETTERS

The apostle Paul wrote nearly half the books in the New Testament (thirteen out of twenty-seven). This accounts for about one third of the New Testament's content. The second most prolific New Testament writer is Luke, followed by the apostle John.

Most of Paul's letters—also called epistles—are to various churches, while the rest are to individuals. The names given to Paul's letters identify the recipient. Paul's thirteen letters are Romans, 1 Corinthians, 2 Corinthians, Galatians, Ephesians, Philippians, Colossians, 1 Thessalonians, 2 Thessalonians, 1 Timothy, 2 Timothy, Titus, and Philemon.

Paul's longer letter to the Romans is covered

separately in *Romans Bible Study*. Similarly, Paul's two letters to the Corinthian church are addressed in the book *Love Is Patient*. Paul's remaining ten books are all shorter and included here.

Six of them are to churches in Galatia, Ephesus, Philippi, Colossae, and Thessalonica (two letters). The others are to individuals: Timothy (two letters), Titus, and Philemon. Though we might expect these books to appear in chronological order of when they were written, this is not the case.

Note that some people attribute the authorship of the book of Hebrews to Paul, while others do not. Hebrews is covered in *Hebrews Bible Study*.

Overall, Paul's writing style carries a more academic feel than the New Testament's other content. This is no doubt a result of his education and training, specifically on the Hebrew Scriptures, which we call the Old Testament.

As a result, expect to see Paul connect the writings of the Old Testament with following Jesus and believing in him. This will give us a richer and deeper understanding of our faith.

Which of Paul's letters do you like best? Which ones are you most looking forward to learning more about?

[Discover more about Paul's writing in 2 Peter 3:15–16.]

[If you're not that familiar with the Bible and how to navigate it, check out the appendix "If You're New to the Bible" for helpful information and background.]

GALATIANS

The book of Galatians is the apostle Paul's letter to Jesus's church in the city of Galatia. Paul has an urgent concern, which prompted his communication to them.

The Bible records Paul making two trips there (Acts 16:6 and Acts 18:23). But it doesn't appear that he stayed long either time, as Scripture gives little details about either visit.

Paul mentions the Galatian churches in his letter to the Corinthians (1 Corinthians 16:1). It's noteworthy that Paul says *churches*, signifying that there's not just one in Galatia, but multiple churches.

Paul's other mention of Galatia is in his second letter to his protégé Timothy, where he notes that

Crescens has gone to Galatia (2 Timothy 4:10). Though Crescens could have gone there on a personal visit, it's more likely Paul sent him there. Though it's speculation, it's possible that Crescens carries with him a dispatch from Paul, possibly even this letter.

Galatians (along with Romans) is a book that has helped shape Christian theology. Among other things, it addresses Christian freedom and faith. It also offers insight into the church's struggle to separate itself from the historical grip of Judaism.

This church—as well as the other churches Paul writes to—has a mix of Jewish and Gentile converts. Their distinct backgrounds serve up some understandably different perspectives on what it means to follow Jesus, as they allow their upbringing to inform how they understand and practice their faith.

Paul seeks to bring them into greater unity.

What information about Galatia surprises you? What are you looking forward to learning from the book of Galatians?

[Discover more about Galatia in 1 Peter 1:1.]

DAY 1: STAY TRUE TO THE GOSPEL
GALATIANS 1

I am astonished that you are so quickly deserting the one who called you to live in the grace of Christ and are turning to a different gospel. (Galatians 1:6)

After his letter's opening, Paul immediately launches into a significant concern he has for the Galatians. He says they're deserting Jesus and turning to a different gospel. We should rightly gasp in horror at this shocking news.

Paul doesn't say how he learned of this, but we know he's astonished by it and how quickly it occurred. We're also not sure what this contrary teaching is. What follows in Paul's letter suggests they're turning to the Jewish law to save them instead of relying solely on Jesus and living in the grace of Christ (such as we see in Galatians 3:5).

In short, they're trying to earn their salvation by obeying the Old Testament rules and not receiving it by grace through Jesus's sacrificial death for their sins. (See Galatians 2:16.)

But the Old Testament law saved no one. It only illustrated that it was impossible for people to earn their right standing with God. The law pointed to the need for a better solution; Jesus is that better solution. In truth, he's the only way for us to be made right with Father God (John 14:6) and receive our salvation.

It would be bad enough if these false teachers were adding other requirements to people putting their faith in Jesus to save them, such as believing in Jesus as step one and then doing something more as step two. That would add to the gospel, which is wrong. (Read parallel warnings not to add to God's words in Proverbs 30:5–6 and Revelation 22:18–19.)

Instead, what these false teachers have proclaimed to the Galatians is even worse—much more so.

These unidentified heretics are teaching Jesus's

followers to turn to a different solution to save them. Paul says they're throwing the people into confusion. Even worse, they're perverting the gospel of Christ. That's harsh language. Yet the people in Galatia are falling for it.

Paul's solution is for them to remember what he told them and not listen to anyone who tries to tell them something different. Paul then explains his source of the true gospel that he taught them.

What steps are people trying to add to salvation today? How should we respond when we encounter this? What should we do if we've fallen victim to any additional salvation requirements? Beyond that, how have we seen the gospel of Jesus perverted today? What should be our response?

[Discover more about the grace of Christ in Romans 5:15, 2 Corinthians 8:9, Ephesians 4:7, and 2 Timothy 1:9. Read Paul's other warning about a different gospel in 2 Corinthians 11:3-4.]

DAY 2: PETER'S ERROR
GALATIANS 2

When Cephas came to Antioch, I opposed him to his face, because he stood condemned. (Galatians 2:11)

After explaining to the Galatians how God called him to preach to them and other Gentiles (that is, all non-Jews), Paul shares about meeting with the apostles in Jerusalem. They confirmed both his message and his call. Peter, also called Cephas, was one of the apostles Paul met with.

Having just name-dropped Peter, it seems strange that Paul moves next to criticize him, but that's exactly what he does.

When Peter (Cephas) went to Antioch, Paul publicly opposed him for what he had done. Here's what happened:

When Peter arrived in Antioch, he ate with the Gentiles. Doing so was contrary to the Jewish people's interpretation of the Old Testament's dietary laws, which was how Peter was raised. But eating with Gentiles, however, is consistent with the freedom we have from the law through Jesus (Romans 10:12). By freely eating with—and associating with—Gentiles, Peter demonstrated God's grace, and one way that Jesus fulfilled the Old Testament law (Matthew 5:17).

Yet when James arrived in Antioch, Peter changed his behavior. He pulled away from the Gentiles. He separated himself from them. Even worse, other Jews—even Barnabas—followed his example. Paul calls this hypocrisy.

Paul attributes Peter's changed behavior to his fear of being criticized by the Jews—specifically "the circumcision group."

The circumcision group were Jewish followers of Jesus who advocated that circumcision was a necessary step for salvation. The church leaders—headed by James, ironically building on Simon

Peter's testimony—decided that circumcision was not a salvation requirement (Acts 15:1–21). What's not clear, however, is which event happened first. But Peter and James were involved both times.

Though Paul rebuffed Peter for his wrong behavior, we don't know Peter's response. We can, however, expect that Peter saw his error and corrected it. May we do the same when we go astray.

What we are privy to is Paul's teaching on the subject.

He reminds us that we aren't justified by obeying the law. No one can be made right with God by following a list of rules. Instead, we're justified when we put our faith in Jesus. Through Jesus, we die to the law and its requirements. This is so that we can live for God. We no longer live for ourselves, but Christ lives in us.

Paul ends by reminding us that if following the law could save us, then Jesus died for nothing.

How do we respond to people who confront our behavior? When have we worried about what other people thought about us? Was this a good concern?

[Discover more about our being one through Jesus in 1 Corinthians 12:13, Galatians 3:28, and Colossians 3:11. Read what Peter writes about hypocrisy in 1 Peter 2:1.]

DAY 3: RECEIVE THE SPIRIT
GALATIANS 3

Did you receive the Spirit by the works of the law, or by believing what you heard? (Galatians 3:2)

In Day 1, we talked about a false teaching that was leading the people astray. As a result, they turned their backs on Jesus and what he had done to save them. Though Paul didn't identify what this errant teaching was, we speculated it was adhering to the Hebrew law to receive their right-eousness, thereby earning their right standing with God. Today's passage tracks with that assumption.

Paul presents them with a rhetorical question. He asks them, when did you receive the Spirit— that is, the Holy Spirit? Did it happen because of your hard work to follow the law? Or did it occur when you believed in Jesus?

It happened, of course, when they said yes to Jesus. That's when they received the Holy Spirit.

Although the Holy Spirit was present and at work in the Old Testament, he only guided select people and often for a limited time. But when Jesus returned to heaven, Father God sent the Holy Spirit to live in everyone who follows Jesus (John 14:16–17 and Acts 2:1–4). This would include all the believers in Galatia.

Paul then launches into an in-depth teaching about the law and its limitations. Quoting the Old Testament—that the people have apparently turned to exclusively—Paul says that everyone who doesn't do everything written in the book of the law is cursed (Deuteronomy 27:26). Since no one can fully obey the Old Testament law, that means everyone is cursed.

If the law could impart life, obeying it would make us fully righteous. But that didn't work then, and it doesn't work now. Instead, we need to turn to Jesus. He—and he alone—can redeem us from the law's curse. We need to come to Jesus in faith to receive what was promised to Abraham, through his seed, which refers to Jesus.

When we come to faith through Jesus, we become children of God. All of us. By putting our faith in Christ, we receive the promise that God gave to Abraham many centuries ago.

Have we fully placed our faith in Jesus to save us, or are we still trying to work our way into heaven? How is the Holy Spirit at work in all of us who follow Jesus? Though we may no longer observe the Old Testament law, what rules have we made up that we try to follow?

[Discover more about the Holy Spirit in John 7:39, Acts 1:8, and Acts 2:38.]

DAY 4: TWO COVENANTS
GALATIANS 4

The women represent two covenants. One covenant is from Mount Sinai and bears children who are to be slaves: This is Hagar. (Galatians 4:24)

We read in the Old Testament of God telling Abraham to travel to another land far away, one that God would show him. God promises Abraham—then called Abram—that he will make him into a great nation (Genesis 12). But Abraham and his wife, Sarah, are childless. For decades, they wait for God's promised son, but it doesn't happen.

Growing desperate, Sarah hatches an ill-conceived plan. She reasons that if she can't provide Abraham with a son, maybe her Egyptian slave can. She gives her handmaiden, Hagar, to Abraham to sleep with. Foolishly, Abraham agrees to his wife's plan. He sleeps with Hagar, and she conceives. She gives birth to Ishmael (Genesis 16).

God's promised plan to Abraham, however, is not to be realized through Ishmael, the son of a slave woman. Instead, it will come through the aging Sarah, who is free.

Years later, when Abraham is one hundred and Sarah is ninety, she miraculously gives birth to a boy —her first and only son. His name is Isaac (Genesis 21:1–7). He is the one from whom God's promise will come. Abraham's offspring will become a great nation through his son Isaac.

Abraham now has two sons. The oldest is Ishmael, the son of Abraham by his wife's slave, Hagar. The younger son is Isaac, son of Abraham and his wife Sarah.

With this as the background, let's apply it to today's reading.

Each woman represents a covenant. Hagar exemplifies the first. It is from Mount Sinai—where God will later give Moses the law. All who are born under this covenant are slaves. Mount Sinai corresponds with the city of Jerusalem, as it existed in

Paul's time. This is because she and her children are in slavery to the law.

Contrast this with Sarah and her son, Isaac, who is the child of God's promise to Abraham. They are free. This corresponds to a future Jerusalem from above. She is our mother, and we are free.

Ishmael was born according to the flesh and is a slave to it. Isaac was born through the power of the Holy Spirit and is free from slavery.

We are not children of the slave woman. Instead, we are children of the free woman, and we will share in that inheritance.

Are those who follow the law slaves to it? Are we free through Abraham's descendant, Jesus? What inheritance will we receive?

[Discover more about the Jerusalem from above in Revelation 21:2 and Revelation 21:9–11.]

DAY 5: WALK BY THE SPIRIT
GALATIANS 5

So I say, walk by the Spirit, and you will not gratify the desires of the flesh. (Galatians 5:16)

Building on Paul's discourse in Galatians 4 on slavery to the law versus freedom through Jesus, chapter 5 begins with a succinct conclusion. Paul says that since we have our freedom through Jesus, we should stand firm, clinging to it. This will keep us from being burdened anew and shackled as slaves (to the law).

Paul represents the law by referencing circumcision. If people who follow Jesus allow themselves to be circumcised, as the law prescribes, then the grace they received through Christ means nothing. If they follow one element of the law, they're obligated to follow the law's complete requirements. This separates them from Jesus.

Though they were once on track in their journey with Jesus and running their race well, they've become distracted. A false teacher has cut in on them and pointed them in a different direction, down the wrong path. Just as circumcision doesn't matter to those who follow Jesus, neither does the Old Testament law.

Instead, we are to rely on God's Spirit, whom Paul mentions eight times in Galatians 5.

Paul writes that we are to walk by the Spirit—that is, the Holy Spirit. Then we will not give in to our human desires. What our body wants opposes what the Spirit calls us to. And the Holy Spirit counters what our flesh wants.

The solution to not give in to our physical cravings is to walk by God's Spirit. The degree to how well we do this is evidenced by what our life produces.

Bad fruit, produced by the acts of the flesh, includes sexual immorality, impurity, debauchery, idolatry, witchcraft, hatred, discord, jealousy, fits of rage, selfish ambition, dissensions, factions, envy, drunkenness, and orgies. This is a long list, and it is far-ranging.

Read these fifteen sins again. This time, however, don't focus on the items that aren't an issue for you. Instead, consider the areas where you struggle.

Yet before you give in to discouragement, realize that as long as we're here on earth, we'll struggle with sin. Paul did. In his letter to the church in Rome, he shares his agony about it. Paul writes that what he wants to do, he doesn't do. And the things he shouldn't do, he does anyway. "What a wretched man I am," he says. But he ends by thanking God, who delivers him through Jesus (Romans 7:15–25). This should be our perspective as well.

As we walk by the Spirit, however, we'll move toward a different result. We'll produce good fruit instead. This is love, joy, peace, forbearance, kindness, goodness, faithfulness, gentleness, and self-control.

As we travel through life, may we walk in the Spirit to move steadily away from producing bad fruit to producing the good fruit that can only come from the Holy Spirit.

Which item on the list of bad fruit weighs us down? How can we better walk by the Spirit to move away from it? Which item on the list of the fruit of the Spirit do we want to embrace more fully? How do we do that?

[Discover more about the desires of the flesh in Romans 8:5, Romans 13:14, Ephesians 2:1–4, and 2 Peter 2:17–19.]

BONUS CONTENT: THE
FRUIT OF THE SPIRIT

The fruit of the Spirit is love, joy, peace, forbearance, kindness, goodness, faithfulness, gentleness and self-control. Against such things there is no law. (Galatians 5:22–23)

When we walk by the Spirit, we will produce the Spirit's fruit. Paul lists nine traits of the fruit of the Spirit. These are not nine different fruits, but one fruit represented in various ways.

The fruit of the Spirit is:

- **Love**: Love is a strong affection and concern toward others. Discover what else Paul says about love in Romans 12:10, Romans 13:8, and 1 Corinthians 13:4–7.

- **Joy**: Joy is an exultant happiness and ecstasy, often coming from God. Read what else Paul writes about joy in Philippians 2:1–2, 1 Thessalonians 3:9, and Philemon 1:7.

- **Peace**: Peace is quiet, calmness, and a lack of hostility. Uncover what else Paul writes about peace in Romans 5:1–2, Romans 12:18, 1 Corinthians 7:15, and Ephesians 4:3.

- **Forbearance**: Forbearance shows tolerance and restraint when provoked. It's being patient. Find what else Paul says about forbearance in Romans 2:4 and Romans 3:25–26. Read about patience in Ephesians 4:2.

- **Kindness**: Kindness is being friendly, nice, generous, sympathetic, and warm-hearted. See what else Paul teaches about kindness in Ephesians 2:7 and Titus 3:4–7.

- **Goodness**: Goodness possesses moral excellence, is upright, and exhibits a positive and desirable nature. Investigate what else Paul teaches about goodness in Romans 15:14 and 2 Thessalonians 1:11.

- **Faithfulness**: Faithfulness is devotion to God, to what we believe, and to others—especially our spouse. Consider what else Paul says about faithfulness in Romans 3:3–4.
- **Gentleness**: Gentleness is considerate, has a kind disposition, and is amiable and tender. Study what else Paul writes about gentleness in Philippians 4:5.
- **Self-Control**: Self-control keeps our desires, emotions, and actions in check. Explore what else Paul has to say about self-control in 1 Corinthians 7:5, 2 Timothy 3:2–5, and Titus 2:6.

Which of the fruit's traits do we see evidenced in our lives? What aspects of the Spirit's fruit do we want to see more of? What should we do about it?

[Discover more about bearing good fruit in Matthew 7:17–20, John 15:16, Romans 7:4, and Colossians 1:9–11. Read another list of positive traits in 2 Peter 1:5–7.]

DAY 6: YOU REAP WHAT YOU SOW
GALATIANS 6

Whoever sows to please their flesh, from the flesh will reap destruction; whoever sows to please the Spirit, from the Spirit will reap eternal life. (Galatians 6:8)

Paul continues talking about living by the flesh versus living by the Spirit. The underlying premise is living in pursuit of the Old Testament law, contrasted with living under Jesus's mercy and grace.

The people who sow to please their flesh do what their selfish, carnal hearts desire. In doing so, they plant seeds. These are not good seeds. Therefore, the crop they produce will not be a good one. The harvest they gather will lead to destruction. They will reap what they sow.

Contrast this with people who sow to please the Spirit. They also plant seeds in the ground. These are good seeds. Therefore, the crop they produce is good. Their harvest will lead to eternal life. They also will reap what they sow.

Does this mean that people who don't sow what pleases the Spirit will not receive Jesus's eternal life?

This certainly is one interpretation. (Consider Ephesians 5:5.) It's a conclusion that should cause us to tremble. It suggests that though we receive Jesus's grace through faith and don't need to earn it, that doesn't guarantee us a trip to heaven when we die. In response to what Jesus did for us, we should strive to be more like him. This is a way for us to thank him and honor him for what he did when he died to save us. As we do this, we sow to please the Spirit.

Another consideration, however, is the size of our harvest. Though all farmers harvest their crops, not all receive the same yield. Some realize a better outcome than others. This could be what Paul means when he talks about reaping eternal life. It's about the size of our harvest. If we sow more, our reward will be greater. If we sow little—or nothing

—we will still join Jesus in heaven, but our reward when we arrive there will be small (Matthew 5:12 and Revelation 22:12).

Regardless of how we interpret what Paul means about reaping eternal life, let's not lose sight of the essential fact that the seeds we sow in this life should be sown to please the Spirit and not ourselves. We should sow seeds for God and his kingdom.

What seeds are we sowing? What type of crop do we expect to reap? How large will our harvest be?

[Discover more about sowing and reaping in Proverbs 11:18 and Matthew 13:23. Read about our reward in Mark 10:29–30.]

EPHESIANS

The book of Ephesians is a letter, or epistle, written by Paul to the church in the city of Ephesus. It's a favorite of many, providing a profound work that offers inspiration and therefore encouragement.

Just as with Galatia, Paul made a missionary stop in Ephesus. Luke details Paul's time there in Acts 18:18–Acts 20:20. Though Paul didn't cause it, his visit even sparked a riot.

We also know that Paul urged Timothy to stay in Ephesus to instruct the people and protect against false doctrines (1 Timothy 1:3–4). Later, Paul sent Tychicus to Ephesus (Ephesians 6:21). Tychicus may have even gone there twice

(2 Timothy 4:12), though these two passages could reference the same trip.

Last, Jesus reveals the truth about the city of Ephesus to John in the apostle's epic vision (Revelation 2:1–7). In this revelation, Jesus affirms the church in Ephesus for not tolerating wicked people, testing those who claimed to be apostles, persevering under hardship, and not giving up.

Yet Jesus has one thing against them. They have forsaken their first love—presumably him. They have fallen far. He urges them to repent of their error or face punishment.

What is most surprising about the church in Ephesus? What can we learn from this overview of them?

[Discover more about Ephesus in 2 Timothy 1:16–18. Read more about Tychicus in Acts 20:4, Colossians 4:7, and Titus 3:12.]

DAY 7: THE SPIRIT OF
WISDOM AND REVELATION
EPHESIANS 1

I keep asking that the God of our Lord Jesus Christ, the glorious Father, may give you the Spirit of wisdom and revelation, so that you may know him better. (Ephesians 1:17)

A recurring theme in many of Paul's letters is how he prays for others. This should encourage us and set an example for us to follow, praying for our family, friends, and those near us.

As confirmed in today's passage, this isn't a single, one-time prayer, but an ongoing request. Paul asks Father God to give the Ephesians the

Spirit of wisdom and revelation. Why is this? So that they will know him better.

Isn't knowing God better something we should all desire and strive for? Of course it is.

First, Paul requests wisdom. Wisdom is more than mere head knowledge of facts and data. Wisdom is the ability to discern how to apply what we know. It allows us to determine what is true, right, and lasting. From our perspective as children of God, wisdom is supernatural insight.

Second, Paul asks for revelation. Revelation is receiving the disclosure of something we hadn't known beforehand. It's a sudden insight. Again, from our spiritual perspective, revelation is receiving supernatural truth.

Paul precedes these two items with the word *Spirit*.

In most versions of the Bible—including the NIV—this is Spirit with a capital S, signifying the Holy Spirit. This means that Paul's request is for the Holy Spirit to give us wisdom and revelation. The Holy Spirit can do that. All we need to do is listen and be open to receive what he reveals.

Other versions of the Bible, however, render spirit with a lowercase s. This changes our under-standing of this passage, as it's not a reference to

God, but to our inner selves. Our spirit is the essence of who we are. Our spirit provides us with an unspoken sense of what is or what will be. Yet isn't God the force behind this as well?

So whether we rely on the Holy Spirit or our internal spirit, which God has placed inside each of us, the result is that we receive wisdom and revelation because of God's work in our lives. Therefore, we shouldn't fixate on whether this is a capital S spirit or a lowercase one.

What we need to focus on is Paul's prayer for God to give us wisdom and revelation. Then we need to be ready to receive it. The purpose of this is so that we'll know God better.

Who can we pray for so they'll receive wisdom and revelation? If we feel we're lacking in either area, what should we do? What can we do to know God better?

[Discover more about wisdom in Matthew 13:54, Luke 2:52, 1 Corinthians 1:20, Colossians 1:28, and James 1:5. Discover more about revelation in 2 Corinthians 12:1 and Galatians 1:12.]

DAY 8: SAVED BY GRACE
EPHESIANS 2

For it is by grace you have been saved, through faith—and this is not from yourselves, it is the gift of God—not by works, so that no one can boast. (Ephesians 2:8–9)

Paul shares a succinct and essential truth about salvation. He tells us how to be saved, which reminds the people in Ephesus of how *they* were saved. This is a bold reminder that salvation is through Jesus alone and not anything else, such as by following the Old Testament law—or any list of dos and don'ts.

Paul writes that we're saved because of God's grace—a good outcome that we don't deserve. We receive this in faith and don't need to work for it—

we can't earn it. Our salvation is a gift from God. As a result, we have no reason to boast in our right standing with God or a sense of accomplishment.

Let's consider these key salvation elements:

By Grace: Our salvation starts with God's grace. Grace gives us what we don't deserve. We don't deserve to be made right with Father God, which comes to us through Jesus when he died in our place for the wrong things we have done.

As we explore how to be saved, it doesn't start with us but with God and his grace.

Through Faith: A second related item is faith. This is our part. We must receive the grace that God offers us through faith. We must believe in Jesus (Romans 10:9). It's that simple.

But this doesn't make sense to most people. It seems too easy. So they pile more requirements upon it, as if making it harder will make it better.

Yet through faith we can receive God's grace. This is how we're saved.

A Gift: Lest there be any doubt, salvation is a gift that God freely gives to us. It's a no-strings-attached present from the Almighty. That's what God's grace does.

Not Works: We can't earn our salvation any

more than we can earn a gift someone's already given us.

Yet when many people consider how to be saved, they think there's a list of requirements they must meet; there's a set of prescribed steps they must go through to earn their salvation.

But we can't work to become eligible to receive a present God's already given us. God's present of salvation—through Jesus—sits before us. All we need to do is open his gift.

How well do we do at truly believing each of these elements in Paul's teaching? If we struggle with any of them, what should we do to better align our thinking with what Scripture teaches?

[Discover more about salvation in John 3:16–17 and Acts 4:12.]

Are you saved? If not—or if you're not sure—why not take this life-altering, all-critical step today? Simply affirm Jesus as Lord and believe God raised him from the dead (Romans 10:9). Don't delay. Do it now.

DAY 9: HOLY SPIRIT POWER
EPHESIANS 3

I pray that out of his glorious riches he may strengthen you with power through his Spirit in your inner being, so that Christ may dwell in your hearts through faith. (Ephesians 3:16–17)

Paul talks a lot about prayer in his letter to the Ephesians. In fact, he mentions prayer in this epistle more times than in any of his other letters. The first three times he talks about how he prays for them (a practice he mentions in several of his other letters). Does this mean they need a lot of prayer or that he's modeling prayer to them? Perhaps both.

Either way, it's not until this chapter's prayer

passage that Paul teaches them about prayer and asks them to pray for him.

In today's reading (specifically Ephesians 3:14–19), Paul gives details about what his prayer for them looks like. He opens by saying that he kneels before the Father. This is his posture for prayer, lowering himself in adoration to make a humble, yet expectant, request.

First, he prays that God will strengthen them through Holy Spirit power. Why is this? So that Jesus will live in their hearts, through faith.

Does this explanation seem strange?

At first it may, but remember that Jesus said that once he returned to heaven, Papa would send the Holy Spirit to his followers in his name. The Holy Spirit would teach them all things, reminding them of everything that Jesus had said (John 14:26).

In this way, we see the Holy Spirit's role in having Jesus live inside us more vibrantly and intensely. Through the power of the Holy Spirit, Jesus takes on a larger existence and a more impactful presence in our lives.

But this is just part one of Paul's prayer. He also prays that we would have power to comprehend the immensity of Jesus's love for us—of how wide, how long, how high, and how deep his love is. Beyond that, Paul wants us to realize that Jesus's love for us is far more important than knowledge.

We don't need to amass information about Jesus. Instead, Paul wants us to know that Jesus's love surpasses knowledge. While there's nothing wrong with learning about Jesus, that pales next to his immense love for us. His love should be our focus.

Why does Paul make this request? It's so that we should be filled to the measure—that is, saturated—with the fullness of God.

May God's love fill us, saturate our being, and overflow from us to others.

How well do we do at letting the Holy Spirit help us embrace Jesus more fully? What does this look like? Are we astounded by Jesus's great love for us? Are we filled to the top and over-flowing with God's fullness?

[Discover Paul's other mentions of prayer in this letter in Ephesians 1:16, Ephesians 1:18, and five times in Ephesians 6:18–20.]

DAY 10: LIVE A LIFE WORTHY
EPHESIANS 4

As a prisoner for the Lord, then, I urge you to live a life worthy of the calling you have received. (Ephesians 4:1)

Paul implores the Ephesians to live in a manner appropriate for their new life with Jesus. He then spends most of the rest of the chapter listing several ways to do that.

As we run through Paul's list of instructions, we need to acknowledge that we aren't doing them to earn our salvation, justify ourselves before our Savior, or cause God to love us more—because we can't. Instead, we do these things out of gratitude to our Lord for what he has already done for us. When we live a life worthy of Jesus, it's a powerful way of thanking him for saving us.

Here are the initial things Paul instructs the Ephesians—and us—to do:

- Be completely humble and gentle (Ephesians 4:2).
- Be patient with one another in love (Ephesians 4:2).
- Strive to live in Holy Spirit unity and peace (Ephesians 4:3).

Unity is an important topic to Paul. He spends the next several verses talking about it, what it entails, and what it produces. To highlight the significance of unity, Paul reminds us that there is one body, one Spirit, one hope, one Lord, one faith, one baptism, and one Father God.

Through Jesus, we are one body, with Christ as our head. Each part of the body has a role to play, forming a whole body that grows and matures in love. But we need unity to make it happen.

After teaching about the importance of unity, Paul continues his instructions for living a worthy life for Jesus:

- Don't behave like the world but remove the old self (Ephesians 4:17, 22).
- Develop a new attitude and put on a new self (Ephesians 4:23–24).
- Don't lie but speak the truth (Ephesians 4:25), which Paul connects back to the unity of being one body.
- Do not sin when angry, thereby giving the devil a foothold into our lives (Ephesians 4:26–27).
- Stop stealing and start working to share with others (Ephesians 4:28).
- Avoid unwholesome talk and instead use words to help others (Ephesians 4:29).
- Don't do anything that distresses the Holy Spirit (Ephesians 4:30).
- Get rid of all bitterness, rage, anger, brawling, slander, and malice (Ephesians 4:31).
- Instead, be kind, compassionate, and forgiving (Ephesians 4:32).

Remember that we don't do these things to get God's attention or earn our salvation. Instead, we pursue them in response to the salvation he's already given us. Then we can live a life worthy of the life Jesus has called us to.

This right living, however, isn't a one-and-done endeavor. It's an ongoing effort that we'll pursue for the rest of our lives. Then, when our time on earth ends, may our Lord welcome us into eternity, saying, "Well done, good and faithful servant!" (Matthew 25:21).

When we do things for God, do we think he'll love us more and esteem us with greater favor? What do we do when we stumble in our efforts to live a life worthy of Jesus? Does our life serve as a huge thank you to Jesus for saving us?

[Discover more about living a worthy life in Philippians 1:27, Colossians 1:10, and 1 Thessalonians 2:12.]

BONUS CONTENT: A PRISONER FOR THE LORD

As a prisoner for the Lord . . . (Ephesians 4:1)

Paul writes to the church in Ephesus from a prison cell. He first mentions his situation in Ephesians 3:1 and now again in Ephesians 4:1. He's likewise incarcerated when he writes to Philemon (Philemon 1:1). Both letters may have been written from the same cell or at different times from different prisons.

In his letters, Paul often calls himself an apostle of Jesus (1 Corinthians 1:1, 2 Corinthians 1:1, Galatians 1:1, Ephesians 1:1, Colossians 1:1, 1 Timothy 1:1, and 2 Timothy 1:1). Another time he identifies himself as a servant of Jesus

(Philippians 1:1) and once as both a servant and an apostle (Titus 1:1).

But it seems his status as a prisoner looms larger for him than being an apostle or servant. Yet, he can be both from behind bars. We see this as he writes letters from jail. This includes his letters to the Ephesians and to Philemon, possibly more.

Being an apostle is something God called Paul to. When he self-identifies as a servant, this is a humble reflection of his relationship to God. Yet his status as a prisoner is something that was forced upon him.

Nevertheless, we see Paul using his time behind bars to encourage and influence others (such as in Acts 28:30–31 and Philippians 1:13–14). In doing so, he does what he can to grow the kingdom of God. As a result, he makes the best of a difficult situation.

When we face trying circumstances we didn't agree to, may we follow Paul's example.

When forced into situations we didn't choose, how can we honor God anyway? As Jesus's followers, what labels do we give ourselves?

[Discover the times Paul mentions being imprisoned for his faith in Jesus in Acts 16:26–28, Acts 23:18, Acts 25:14, Acts 25:27, Acts 27:1, Philippians 1:14, Colossians 4:10, 2 Timothy 1:8, and Philemon 1:9–13.]

DAY 11: SUBMIT
EPHESIANS 5:1–6:9

Submit to one another out of reverence for Christ.
(Ephesians 5:21)

Submit is not a popular word among people today. To submit means to yield to the will, authority, or power of someone else. In military terms it means to *come under the mission*. We can extend this to our faith, as we come under the mission of Jesus.

Few people want to submit to anyone or anything. Most seek to please themselves without regard for the position of others.

Yet Paul tells us to submit.

First, we are to submit to God (James 4:7). We

know that. We likely even agree with it, but we may have trouble following through. Yet we are to submit to God. This starts with doing what he tells us to do in the Bible.

Speaking of Scripture, the Bible also says we're to submit to every human authority (1 Peter 2:13–15). This is harder to do. What if we disagree with them? Or what if they're evil? What if they oppose Jesus and all who stand with him? Yet Peter doesn't give any exceptions. He just tells us to submit to human authority.

Next, Paul tells us to submit to one another. We do so out of respect for Jesus and to venerate him. This type of submission may be even harder to do, but God commands us to do so through his Word, so we should do it.

To help us move forward, Paul lists common situations where it's important to submit. It's a challenging list, one that many people struggle with. Let's cover the most controversial one first.

Wives are to submit to their husbands, just as they do to God. Paul teaches that the husband is the head of the house, just as Jesus is the head of the church. As the church submits to Jesus, wives should submit to their husbands.

This is not an accepted idea today, not at all.

But just because popular opinion opposes it doesn't mean we can dismiss what the Bible teaches.

Next, husbands are to love their wives. This may be how husbands can best submit to them. The love of husbands for their wives should parallel Jesus's love for us. Paul then devotes seven more verses to explain how and why. This suggests he carries more concern about husbands loving their wives than wives submitting to their husbands.

Third, Paul addresses children. They are to obey their parents. They're to submit to what their parents tell them to do. The Ten Commandments say to honor our fathers and mothers (Exodus 20:12 and Deuteronomy 5:16). When we do, we will receive favor and enjoy a long life.

Now Paul switches back to men, this time addressing them as fathers instead of husbands. They are not to exasperate their children. Instead, they should teach them about God.

Fifth, Paul addresses slaves. Their form of submission is to obey their earthly masters. This means to do what they're told, not run away, and not steal. Though few of us live in this type of slavery today, we'll do well to adopt this same posture with our employers.

Finally, Paul talks to masters, which we could

extend to cover bosses. They're to treat their charges well and not threaten them.

Paul's six examples of submission address wives, husbands, children, fathers, slaves (or employees), and masters (or employers). We all fit in one category, likely more. May Paul's instructions guide us in how to best submit to one another.

How well do we do in submitting to God? What about every human authority? Which of Paul's six examples of submitting do we need to do better at?

[Discover other times Paul says to submit in Romans 13:5 and 1 Corinthians 16:15–16. Read a parallel passage in Colossians 3:18–4:1.]

DAY 12: THE FULL ARMOR OF GOD
EPHESIANS 6

Therefore put on the full armor of God, so that when the day of evil comes, you may be able to stand your ground, and after you have done everything, to stand. (Ephesians 6:13)

Paul tells us to put on the full armor of God. To the casual reader, this might seem like a call to pick up arms or an incitement for military action. It's not. It's spiritual.

This is a visual aid to help people remember key items needed to prevail in spiritual conflict. These are truth, righteousness, sharing the gospel, faith, salvation, and the word of God.

To visualize this, Paul paints a word picture

using a Roman soldier, which his readers would have been most familiar with. Paul connects a soldier's essential gear with these key spiritual elements. To recall Paul's six items, readers need only to envision a soldier in uniform and associate each spiritual element with its physical counterpart. They are:

- **Belt**: *truth*. Today we wear a belt to hold our pants up. In Paul's day, a belt held free-flowing garments closer to the body, making it easier to move quickly. This is what truth—God's truth—does. It makes it easier for us to be ready to move forward for him.
- **Breastplate**: *righteousness*. Our righteousness—that is, our right living—protects our heart from the assaults of the enemy. When we do wrong, our adversary has an opening to attack us. When we do what's right, it's harder for him to launch an assault.
- **Shoes**: *a readiness to share the gospel of peace*. We put on shoes to go for a walk. As we move about, we should be ready to share God's good news with everyone

we meet. Shoes are a reminder to be ready.

- **Shield**: *faith.* Just as a breastplate covers our chest, a shield protects our body. In the same way, right living protects our heart, while faith protects our whole being.

- **Helmet**: *salvation.* A soldier's helmet protects his head, which not only holds most of his senses—sight, sound, smell, and taste—but also provides the knowledge of how to fight. For us, our salvation through Jesus is what protects us. Without him, nothing else matters.

- **Sword**: *the word of God.* The sword is the only offensive tool of the group. Paul identifies the sword as representing the word of God. Though we commonly think of the word of God as referring to the Bible, remember that the New Testament didn't exist when Paul wrote this. Though he could mean the Hebrew Scriptures, it's more likely he's referring to the *spoken* word of God, which comes to us from the Holy Spirit. The Holy Spirit can guide us in what to do and say

when we're under attack (Luke 12:11–
12).

Paul's reference to the armor of God is not
about a physical battle, which many people have
missed throughout the ages. Instead, it's a spiritual
conflict that followers of Jesus must be prepared to
engage in. In doing so, they use truth, righteousness, the gospel, faith, salvation, and the word
of God.

This is what putting on the armor of God
reminds us of.

How can we best view the armor of God? Which item is our
strength? Which one do we need to work on?

[Discover a parallel passage in 1 Thessalonians 5:7–
8.]

PHILIPPIANS

The apostle Paul wrote the book of Philippians to the church in the city of Philippi.

The book of Philippians is Paul's most joy-filled letter. This is despite him struggling with hardship and opposition.

The word *joy*, along with *rejoice*, occurs frequently throughout this letter. This results in an encouraging and uplifting text that celebrates faith and the confidence that we can have from following Jesus.

Paul went to Philippi twice.

Paul's first visit lasted several days. While there, Paul was imprisoned for casting a spirit out of a female slave. God used an earthquake to free Paul from jail. The result was that the jailer and his family were saved (Acts 16:11–40). The city officials then urged Paul and his team to leave. Not surprisingly, Paul later wrote that he had suffered and was treated outrageously in Philippi (1 Thessalonians 2:2).

Paul's second visit to Philippi was even shorter; this time it was uneventful (Acts 20:6).

When Paul writes this letter, it's with the thought that he may return (Philippians 1:27). But Scripture doesn't record a third visit.

DAY 13: LIVE FOR CHRIST
PHILIPPIANS 1

For to me, to live is Christ and to die is gain. (Philippians 1:21)

Paul reveals his perspective on life and death. It's inspiring and worthy of emulation. It's a holistic, God-centered view. In it, Paul shares his outlook for what lay ahead. It has life and death significance.

In many of his letters—including this one—Paul identifies as being a servant of Jesus Christ. This is an amazing and inspiring objective. May we adopt it as our own. As long as Paul lives, he will do so for Christ. Serving Jesus is his reason for living, life purpose, and primary goal.

As a servant of Jesus, everything Paul does is for his Savior. He tells others about Christ, encourages them to turn their lives over to Jesus, and teaches them how to grow in their faith. To Paul, Jesus matters more than anything, and all else comes after that.

In his second letter to the Corinthians, Paul details what he has suffered to serve his Savior (2 Corinthians 11:22–27). This includes being imprisoned, flogged, lashed thirty-nine times (on five separate occasions), beaten, stoned, ship-wrecked three times, often endangered, deprived of sleep, hungry and thirsty, even cold and naked.

Paul endured all this so he could boldly proclaim Jesus. He'll continue serving Jesus as long as he is alive. His labor will produce fruit for God's kingdom.

It's an awe-inspiring example that we will do well to follow.

Much later in life, Paul writes to Timothy. Paul tells his protégé that he has fought the good fight. He has finished his race. He has kept his faith (2 Timothy 4:7). Paul says he finished strong.

The alternative to life is death.

Yet Paul doesn't see death as the end. He sees it as a wonderful continuation of his existence, the culmination. In dying, Paul expects to gain even more. He anticipates living forever with Jesus. Oh, how he longs to realize that.

Paul lives in tension between continuing to serve his Savior and going to live with him forever. The first pales in comparison to the second.

Yet he acknowledges it's better for the Philippians—and implicitly many others—if he remains on earth longer. That way he can help them grow in their faith.

Life is finite, while eternal life is infinite. No matter how much life we have to live here on earth, when we die, we face an infinite existence, regardless of when we begin it.

However many days we have left, may we be like Paul and fight the good fight, finish our race, and keep our faith. May we finish strong. As we do so, let us inspire and encourage others on their faith journey.

What are we doing to live for Christ? Do we look forward to death or fear it? What do we need to focus on for the rest of our time on Earth?

[Discover people who didn't die in Genesis 5:24, 2 Kings 2:11, and possibly John 21:22–23. Read about the alternative in 1 Thessalonians 4:17.]

DAY 14: WORK OUT YOUR SALVATION
PHILIPPIANS 2

Continue to work out your salvation with fear and trembling, for it is God who works in you to will and to act in order to fulfill his good purpose. (Philippians 2:12–13)

When Paul tells the church of Philippi to work out their salvation, he doesn't say to work *for* it. They've already received eternal life as a free gift through God's goodness (his grace), and there's nothing they need to do to earn it. (See Day 8.)

Jesus died in our place and took on our punishment for all the things we've done wrong. In doing so, he made us right with Father God. It's a gift he gives us with no expectations, restrictions, or obligations.

What do we do when someone gives us a gift? We show our appreciation. This starts with saying thank you, and we might follow up with a note or card. Depending on the gift, we may proudly wear it, use it, or display it for all to see. In doing so, we honor the giver.

If we follow Jesus as his disciple, he's given us the ultimate gift that anyone could ever give. It's the gift of salvation through him and eternal life with him.

This deserves the best thank you we could ever offer. This isn't a one-and-done show of appreciation; it warrants ongoing, lifelong gratitude.

Receiving the greatest gift—one that will last the rest of our lives here on earth and forever into eternity—warrants that we say thank you every day. We do this with our words, thoughts, and actions, making sure they align with God's instructions in the Bible and his will for our life.

This is how we work out our salvation. This is how we honor the Giver.

Working out our salvation isn't a requirement, but it is an appropriate response. It's a show of gratitude for what Jesus has done for us, and we should want to live a changed life as an ongoing display of appreciation.

So that we don't dismiss this as a trivial task, Paul tells us to work out our salvation with fear and trembling. This trepidation isn't because God could take back his gift; it's a reflection of his almighty power, which we should be in awe of and never take for granted.

What immediately follows Paul's instruction to work out our salvation is a great place to start. He says to do everything without grumbling or arguing. This will help us become blameless and pure.

We don't have to work out our salvation, but we should want to, because eternal life is a gift that surpasses all others.

How are we working out our salvation? Should we be doing more to thank our Savior for what he did for us? How can we do so with a feeling of appreciation and not obligation?

[Discover more about thanking God in Psalm 136:1, Ephesians 5:20, and 1 Thessalonians 5:18.]

DAY 15: PRESS ON
PHILIPPIANS 3

But one thing I do: Forgetting what is behind and straining toward what is ahead, I press on toward the goal to win the prize for which God has called me heavenward in Christ Jesus. (Philippians 3:13–14)

In Day 13 we talked about living for Christ. In day 14, we talked about working out our salvation. Now we'll continue the theme with another important verse in Paul's letter. He again shares his personal perspective, just as he did in Philippians 1:21.

Paul writes that he forgets the past and strains toward the future. He presses on in pursuit of the goal to win the heavenly prize that God calls him to.

First, Paul forgets what's behind him. Paul did some despicable things earlier in his life (1 Timothy 1:13). He persecuted followers of Jesus, imprisoning them and even advocating their deaths. He hunted them down, intending to rid the world of their presence (Acts 26:9–11). Though he can't undo what he did, he can work to move beyond it, turning his negative past into a positive future.

Isaiah also tells us to forget what was and not dwell on the past (Isaiah 43:18). We should follow Isaiah's instruction and Paul's example if we want to move forward with our lives. We cannot let the past weigh us down (Ezekiel 33:10). It's a requirement if we are to make progress.

With our past securely left in our rearview mirror, we can focus on whatever is before us. We don't sit idly in the present, and we don't coast forward. We strain toward what is ahead.

This requires intentional effort. We do what we can with our God-given abilities, all the while knowing that it won't be enough. We do what we can and depend on our Lord for the rest. This is how we can best strain toward tomorrow.

In forgetting the past and straining toward the

future, Paul presses on toward the goal. We should follow his example, realizing that not all forward movement is good. Instead, we must have an objective in mind. Paul's anticipation was of winning the prize of God calling him home when his time here on earth was over. May we all receive this prize at the end of our earthly lives.

Jesus also had this intentional drive to press on (Luke 13:33). He had a purpose for coming to earth; it was to save us. He pressed on to reach that goal, which was to suffer for us, dying for our sins so we wouldn't have to.

Jesus pressed on and so did Paul. We should follow their examples and strive to do the same.

How is our past holding us back? What must we do to leave it behind? What are we straining to do for our Lord? Do we anticipate the prize of God calling us home?

[Discover more about running to get a prize in 1 Corinthians 9:24–27. Read more about the need to press on in Hosea 6:3.]

DAY 16: REJOICE IN THE LORD
PHILIPPIANS 4

Rejoice in the Lord always. I will say it again: Rejoice!
(Philippians 4:4)

In our introduction to Paul's letter, we noted that the book of Philippians is Paul's most joy-filled epistle. He uses the word *joy* five times and *rejoice* eight times in six verses, for a combined total of thirteen. This is more joy and rejoicing than in any of Paul's other letters.

Rejoice even makes two appearances in today's verse. This amplifies Paul's command for us to rejoice. He also uses the word rejoice twice in Philippians 1:18, which likewise adds emphasis to his attitude of rejoicing.

We already noted that Paul has no human reason to rejoice, as detailed in 2 Corinthians 11:22–27. Yet he does so anyway. So should we. He says so—twice in today's verse alone.

What follows Paul's emphatic command for us to rejoice are three ways we may move toward an attitude of joy, rejoicing over our situation to our Lord.

Paul says to let our gentleness be clear to all. Even if we're not naturally gentle, we should strive —with God's help—to move in that direction. In doing so we can rejoice; so can the recipients of our gentleness.

Next Paul tells us not to be anxious about anything. That is, don't worry. Instead, in every situation we turn to God in prayer. We present our requests to him, coupled with thanksgiving. Depending on God for help and having a thankful heart are other reasons to rejoice.

The third part of Paul's instruction is where we should allow our thoughts to dwell. This is on anything excellent or praiseworthy. The list includes what is true, noble, right, pure, lovely, and admirable.

Focusing on the positive will allow us to naturally overflow with rejoicing. Focusing on the negative, however, will have the opposite effect. What we think about can give us joy or rob us of it.

Paul also talks about rejoicing in Philippians 2:17–18. He sees a reason to rejoice and asks the Philippians to rejoice with him. A few verses later Paul repeats his command to rejoice in the Lord (Philippians 3:1).

May we learn from Paul's example and likewise rejoice in the Lord.

Are we more likely to rejoice or to complain? Does our rejoicing encourage others? How do we think God receives our rejoicing?

[Discover what else Paul says about rejoicing in Romans 12:15, 2 Corinthians 13:11, and 1 Thessalonians 5:16–18. Read some of the verses where Paul talks about joy in this letter in Philippians 1:4, Philippians 2:2, and Philippians 4:1.]

BONUS CONTENT: ALL THINGS

I can do all this through him who gives me strength.
(Philippians 4:13)

Paul makes the bold statement that he can do all things through God who gives him strength. Is this claim unique to Paul, or does it apply to us as well?

Many people strive to accomplish things under their own power. Though this sometimes works for them, at least for a while, they come to a point where they reach the end of their abilities. They can give up or turn to God for the needed strength to press on.

Even better would be for them to turn to God at

the beginning of their project and not wait until they had exhausted all their own capabilities.

Our reliance on God honors him, but we disrespect him when we try to push forward on our own.

Yet our Lord seldom rescues us when we haven't asked for his help and strength. He often allows us to flounder on our own until we recognize the need to turn to him for help.

In another letter, Paul says he delights in the face of difficulties and opposition. He writes, "For when I am weak, then I am strong" (2 Corinthians 12:10). We can be weak on our own or strong through the Lord.

With God on our side, we can do all things through him who gives us strength.

Do we truly say that we can do all things through God who gives us strength? When we feel weak, what should we do?

[Discover more about God giving us strength in Psalm 18:1, Psalm 22:19, Psalm 28:7, Psalm 29:11, Psalm 105:4, and Psalm 118:14.]

COLOSSIANS

The apostle Paul wrote the book of Colossians to the church in the city of Colossae.

The main purpose of the book of Colossians is to counteract a heresy—that is, a false teaching — that crept into the church. It's imperative to Paul that he address this before they fall even further from the core belief of salvation through Jesus and him alone.

This heresy may have involved adding human tradition and spirituality to faith in Jesus (Colossians 2:8). This may have included angel worship (Colossians 2:18) and following manmade rules (Colossians 2:20).

Despite its brevity, Paul's letter to the Colossians

contains many profound passages that give us much to consider.

Scripture does not record Paul ever going to Colossae; the Bible's only mention of the city is in Colossians 1:2.

DAY 17: PLEASE THE LORD
COLOSSIANS 1

Live a life worthy of the Lord and please him in every way: bearing fruit in every good work, growing in the knowledge of God. (Colossians 1:10)

In Day 14, we talked about Paul's instruction to work out our salvation. This wasn't to work *for* our salvation, which we've already received. It's in response to our salvation, a way of saying thank you to Jesus for the ultimate gift he gave us.

Today's passage carries a parallel thought. We are to live a life worthy of our Lord. We don't live a worthy life to receive special favor or garner God's attention. Instead, we live a worthy life in reaction to what Jesus has already done for us. (See Day 10.)

In short, we aspire to do better because of Jesus's gift of salvation. We do this by living a life worthy of our Lord.

Consider the situation. Jesus died in our place, receiving the punishment for all the bad things we have ever done and ever will do; he atones for all our sins—past, present, and future. In this way, he saves us. All we need to do is accept it. Our salvation through Jesus makes us right with Father God. We become part of his kingdom, both here on earth now and in heaven after our physical body dies.

In view of all that Jesus did for us, we respond by living a life worthy of him who made the ultimate sacrifice for us. A worthy life shows our appreciation to our Savior. It tells him thank you in the most dramatic fashion.

Living a worthy life for the Lord pleases him in every way. As we've already said, we don't do this to earn anything or to get his attention. Instead, we do it just because of all that he has already done for us.

Living a life worthy of Jesus produces two outcomes.

The first result is to bear fruit in every good

work. These good works aren't to save us (Ephesians 2:8–9). These good works are to point people to Jesus so they will accept the saving work he has already done for them. In this way, we bear fruit, producing a harvest of thirty, sixty, or even a hundredfold (Matthew 13:23).

The other result is to grow in knowledge of God. We seek to know him more fully. We do this when we spend time with him. This includes talking with him through prayer, listening to the Holy Spirit, and reading his Word. We can also grow in knowledge of God through our fellowship with other believers (Hebrews 10:24–25). As the proverb says, iron sharpens iron (Proverbs 27:17).

When we live a worthy life for our Lord, we'll bear fruit and grow in knowledge.

How are we doing in living a life worthy of our Lord? What fruit are we bearing? How are we growing in our knowledge of God?

[Discover Paul's other verses about living a worthy life in Ephesians 4:1, Philippians 1:27, and

1 Thessalonians 2:11–12. Consider people who viewed themselves as unworthy in Job 40:4, Luke 3:16, Luke 7:7, and 1 Corinthians 15:9.]

DAY 18: DON'T LET ANYONE JUDGE YOU
COLOSSIANS 2

Therefore do not let anyone judge you by what you eat or drink, or with regard to a religious festival, a New Moon celebration or a Sabbath day. (Colossians 2:16)

Today's verse opens with the helpful word *therefore*. Whenever we see *therefore*, we're reminded to see what it's there for. That means looking at what precedes it to gain critical context for what follows it.

The passage that leads up to today's verse talks about our salvation through Jesus, baptism, and spiritual circumcision. He forgave our sins and canceled our legal indebtedness to him, taking it away.

Therefore—because of what Jesus did for us and our right standing through him—we should let no one judge us for what we eat and drink, for how we regard various days and celebrations. These Old Testament rules and festivals anticipated what was to come, which we now find fulfilled with Jesus. That means they don't apply anymore.

Yet some people today hold these things with unwarranted importance. This causes them to evaluate others. They judge people for what they eat or don't eat. They judge people for what they drink or don't drink. Last, they judge people for how they treat Old Testament commands for certain days and celebrations.

As a result, some people judge others who consume alcohol, while others judge those who abstain. Then there are many judgments about diet and consumption. Paul says this is a nonissue (Romans 14:3).

Where we mostly see this judgment come from today is in how people regard the Sabbath. They critically judge—and even condemn—those who hold views counter to their own.

This includes which day is the Sabbath. Is it our Saturday? Is it our Sunday? Does it even matter? It also addresses what we do or don't do on the Sabbath. Some adhere to the Old Testament law (Exodus 31:15), others follow God's creation example to rest on the seventh day and treat it as holy (Genesis 2:2–3), while others dismiss it, treating it like any other day (Romans 14:5).

Regardless, we should do what we feel is right and not let others cause us to do what we feel is wrong. In this way, we must be fully convinced in our own minds.

Notice that Paul doesn't tell us not to judge others for these things (though that would be a wise move). Instead, he says not to let anyone else judge us.

We can't control others who look down on us, but we can control how we react to their criticism. Our response to receiving unwanted judgment about these issues should be to ignore it. This is the best way to not let anyone else judge us over these matters.

How have we judged others over food, drink, or the Sabbath? How have others judged us for these things? Have we given in to their unwanted and unhealthy judgment or dismissed it?

[Discover more about judgment in Leviticus 19:15, Luke 6:37, and 1 Corinthians 4:3–5.]

DAY 19: SET YOUR HEART ON THINGS ABOVE
COLOSSIANS 3

Set your hearts on things above. (Colossians 3:1)

Paul tells all who have salvation through Christ to set their *hearts* on things above. This is where Jesus waits for us, sitting on the right hand of God. And this is where we will one day be, when our time here on earth is over.

In the next verse, Paul tells us to set our *minds* on things above, not to think about earthly things.

Which is it, our hearts or our minds?

It's both.

Consider that the things our hearts desire relate to emotions. We need to direct our passions heavenward. We can't let our feelings control us or dictate our thoughts and behavior. That's why we need to focus our emotions on Jesus. May our hearts long to live for him, to die for him, and to be with him. Let us fix our emotions and their outcomes on Jesus (Hebrews 3:1).

Next is our minds. Our minds relate to intellect. It's what we know. We are to direct our accumulation of knowledge heavenward as well. Knowing Jesus should be more important than knowing anything else (Philippians 3:8).

In the verses that follow these dual commands, Paul gives practical tips on how to turn our hearts and our minds toward Jesus in heaven.

First, because we have a new life in Jesus, we must put to death our old way of living. These things make up our earthly nature. Topping the list is sexual immorality, followed by impurity, lust, evil desires, and greed (Colossians 3:5).

We must also push aside anger, rage, malice, slander, and filthy language (Colossians 3:8).

Relating to our language, we shouldn't lie to each other. We must take off falsehood like removing a set of old clothes that we will toss aside. In its place, we should put on our new self, knowing that we are being renewed in God's image (Colossians 3:9-10).

Continuing the clothing metaphor, we are to cover ourselves with compassion, kindness, humility, gentleness, and patience (Colossians 3:12).

We're to tolerate others and forgive them (Colossians 3:13). We cap all these virtues with love, which interconnects them to produce a unified response (Colossians 3:14).

With all these specific qualities to guide us, we can summarize them with the principle that whatever we do or say, we should do so in Jesus's name, giving thanks to Father God (Colossians 3:17).

In this way, we set our hearts and minds on things above.

What do we set our hearts on? What do we set our minds on? What should we do in Jesus's name that we aren't already doing?

[Discover other things Paul says about our thinking in Romans 13:14, Galatians 6:3, and Philippians 4:8.]

DAY 20: PRAYER PRIORITY
COLOSSIANS 4

Devote yourselves to prayer, being watchful and thankful.
(Colossians 4:2)

Paul tells us to devote ourselves to prayer. He doesn't say merely to pray. He says to devote ourselves to its practice. To devote ourselves means to give it our all, to make it our priority.

The word *pray*, and its variations, appears in most books in the Bible. It shows up in hundreds of verses, giving us a lot of insight and information about praying.

In this specific teaching, Paul says in our devotion to prayer to be watchful and thankful.

But what does it mean to be watchful? Though *watchful* is the most common rendering in various Bible translations, another frequent alternative is *being alert*. A third thought addresses *vigilance*.

Consider a guard in a watchtower, scanning the horizon for danger. Though the lookout will sound an alarm when danger approaches, our response when we spot a threat is to turn to God in prayer. This is an example of being watchful.

We don't want to let the enemy catch us off guard and attack us unaware. Instead, we watch so that we can pray at the first sign of an approaching problem.

Therefore, our devotion to prayer begins with being watchful. We don't let our guard down. We remain alert, diligently scanning the horizon for approaching danger.

Next, Paul says we should be thankful.

Though we rightly know that thanksgiving is an important part of prayer, it's much harder to put into practice. The default stance with most prayers is to think about what we need and want. Though we are right to present our requests to God, we are in error to do only that. Instead, we should cover our prayers with thanksgiving (Philippians 4:6).

After Paul's instruction to the Colossian church

to devote themselves to prayer, he asks them to pray for him and his ministry. Praying for the needs of others is a sure antidote to praying only for our personal issues. Though there's nothing wrong with praying about what makes us anxious and causes us to worry, it shouldn't be the only reason we pray.

Later in his letter, Paul holds up Epaphras as an example of one who wrestles in prayer (Colossians 4:12). The idea of wrestling in prayer is an apt image of someone who devotes themselves to prayer.

Let us take Paul's instructions seriously and find encouragement through Epaphras's example.

Does Paul's command to devote ourselves to prayer encourage us or discourage us? How can we be more watchful in prayer? How can we be more mindful to include thankfulness when we talk to God?

[Discover more teaching from Paul about prayer in Romans 8:26, Ephesians 6:18, 1 Thessalonians 5:16–18, and 1 Timothy 2:1.]

1 THESSALONIANS

The apostle Paul wrote the book of 1 Thessalonians to the church in the city of Thessalonica. The letter lists three senders: Paul, Silas, and Timothy. It's likely Paul took the lead on this, with Silas and Timothy voicing their agreement or possibly providing input.

Paul made one missionary visit to Thessalonica (Acts 17:1–10). He stayed there for at least three weeks, persuading many to follow Jesus.

But some Jews were jealous of Paul's impact on the people. They recruited some rascals to form a mob and start a riot. That night, the people sent Paul to another city. Paul later affirms the church in Philippi for sending him aid while he was in Thessalonica (Philippians 4:16).

First Thessalonians is perhaps Paul's most affectionate letter, often tenderly calling them brothers and sisters. He writes as a loving, gentle, and caring father, who seeks to support and nurture the young church in that city.

The central theme of Paul's letter is to encourage this church—and by extension—all followers of Jesus) to stand firm in their faith amid opposition, continuing to grow toward spiritual maturity, that is, to pursue a deeper understanding of God and our relationship to him.

DAY 21: BE A MODEL
1 THESSALONIANS 1

And so you became a model to all the believers in Macedonia and Achaia. (1 Thessalonians 1:7)

Paul affirms the church in Thessalonica for being a model to the believers in the area. He notes they had imitated him and his fellow missionaries. Though this could refer to all who traveled with him, it could also mean him, Silas, and Timothy—the senders of this letter.

Regardless, the Thessalonians' willingness to imitate Paul and his crew had a profound ripple effect. Their God-honoring example allowed them to become a model throughout the area. Because of the noteworthy way they conducted themselves as followers of Jesus, Paul's message of salvation spread throughout the entire region.

Beyond that, Paul writes that their faith in God has become known everywhere. That's an astounding impact.

By imitating Paul, the Thessalonians had a positive effect on the people who lived in the surrounding towns and countryside. As a result, they pointed people to Jesus.

This idea of them imitating Paul and how he lived out his faith isn't unique to the Thessalonian people. In Paul's first letter to the church in Corinth, he tells them to do just that. He urges them to imitate him (1 Corinthians 4:16).

Telling someone to copy everything we do seems like a bold, even arrogant, statement. Yet it makes sense for Paul to do so.

Jesus often told people to follow him. These people could see him and were with him. If Paul were to tell the people in Thessalonica (or Corinth) to follow Jesus and be like him, they wouldn't know what to do. They'd never seen Jesus in action and would be clueless about what he did or how he behaved.

Paul was around Jesus, even though he didn't follow him at the time. Paul also received divine revelations from the Lord (2 Corinthians 12:1–7). Since Paul knows Jesus and how to follow him, it makes sense that the Thessalonians could imitate Paul, as he imitates Jesus.

Later in the same letter to the Corinthians, Paul is more direct, clearing up any doubt we may have. He says, "Follow my example, just as I follow Jesus's" (1 Corinthians 11:1).

May we live a life worthy of imitation. As we live for Jesus, may our lives serve as a model for others to follow.

How well do we do at following Jesus's example? Is our life a model that others can imitate? Does the life we live impact those around us with the good news of Jesus?

[Discover more about following Jesus in Mark 1:17, Luke 9:23, and John 10:27. Read more about Paul's example in 2 Thessalonians 3:7–10.]

DAY 22: PLEASE GOD
1 THESSALONIANS 2–3

We are not trying to please people but God, who tests our hearts. (1 Thessalonians 2:4)

Paul pointedly tells the Thessalonians that he and his group are not trying to please people. Instead, their goal is to please God. The Almighty knows their motives and tests their hearts accordingly. His opinion matters. It's all that matters.

We should likewise strive to please God. Yet this is often a struggle. When people criticize what we do, it's our default nature to react to that criticism. We may attempt to explain our situation or apologize for what we said or did. We may even change our behavior to avoid criticism in the future.

In some circumstances these reactions are appropriate. We made a mistake and must salvage the situation and correct our error.

But other times, even though we did nothing wrong—nothing that displeases our Lord—we act as though we did. We explain, grovel, or alter our behavior to offset the criticism we received. We are people pleasers. Instead, we should strive to be God pleasers. His judgment is the only view that should concern us.

Too often I see ministers fall into this error. Someone criticizes them for their Sunday sermon, even though it was biblically based and appropriately delivered. Despite the reality that their message was God-honoring, they reacted to the perceived slight with an apology. From then on, they guard their words more carefully, even to the point of toning down the Word of God. They don't want to offend anyone anymore.

This doesn't mean that we don't do the same thing. It's just that ministers are in a much more visible position, making it easier for us to see when they fall into the trap of trying to please people.

Yet this issue can go beyond criticism. Sometimes the concern escalates into a confrontation. This happened to Jesus often. It also occurred throughout the early church. Paul was often at the center of these confrontations.

Beyond confrontation comes outright persecution.

More than once the people tried to stone Jesus (John 8:59 and John 10:31). In the end, the Jewish leaders brought about Jesus's execution. Likewise, Stephen was martyred (Acts 7:57–58). Paul also faced great persecution (2 Corinthians 11:23–25). This included being imprisoned, beaten, flogged, whipped, and stoned. History tells us he died for his faith, as did the other disciples.

Whether we face criticism, confrontation, or outright persecution for how we live our lives for Jesus, may we not worry about what others think, say, or do. Our only concern should be what our Lord—who tests our hearts—concludes.

Instead of trying to please people, we should strive to please God—and only him.

What do we do when people wrongly criticize us? Is that the best response? Are we more of a people pleaser or a God pleaser?

[Discover more about pleasing God in Romans 8:8, 1 Thessalonians 4:1, and Hebrews 11:6.]

DAY 23: BE SANCTIFIED
1 THESSALONIANS 4

It is God's will that you should be sanctified: that you should avoid sexual immorality. (1 Thessalonians 4:3)

Paul writes that it's God's will for us to be sanctified. Sanctified means we're set apart for God and consecrated, becoming holy and being made pure. Though we might think that to be sanctified means to be perfect, it does not. Yet our ongoing sanctification moves us in that direction.

Sanctification is a New Testament concept. The word doesn't appear in the Old Testament. Also interesting is that half of its fourteen occurrences are in Paul's letters, three times to the church in Thessalonica and twice in 1 Thessalonians alone.

Sanctification starts with Jesus. It's that simple, and it's that true. Don't forget this.

In his lengthy prayer before his crucifixion, Jesus asks Father God to sanctify his disciples. Then Jesus says that he will sanctify himself, which will allow for their sanctification (John 17:17–19). If Jesus's death sanctified his disciples, is there any reason to suspect he hasn't likewise sanctified us?

When we commit ourselves to follow Jesus, we become spiritually sanctified at that moment. In God's eyes, we are made right with him through Jesus's sacrificial death. Yet in our physical reality, this is not the case. Our bodies aren't sanctified right away. Instead, we merely move in that direction—or at least we should.

Paul gives a practical way to move toward the spiritual sanctification that we've already received. He says to avoid sexual immorality.

Sexual immorality is any behavior that falls outside of the accepted norms. Yet we'd be wrong to interpret this from the attitude of today's anything-goes society. Instead, we must define sexual immorality as was the case when the Bible was written. The Bible says a lot about the subject in very exacting detail.

The Scriptural view of sexual immorality is any sexual behavior that falls outside of a monogamous marriage between a man and a woman. We must avoid all other sexual activity. We do this by controlling our own bodies and not giving in to passionate lust. God calls us to live a holy life, not to wallow in impurity (1 Thessalonians 4:7).

Paul says that anyone who rejects this instruction rejects God. Pause and contemplate this.

Living a sexually moral life is an essential part of our ongoing sanctification.

Paul's second use of the word sanctify in this letter occurs as he concludes it. He proclaims a blessing, that God will sanctify them through and through (1 Thessalonians 5:23).

May we also receive this blessing.

How well do we do in seeing sanctification as an ongoing process? How can we live a life that's set apart for God, consecrated, holy, and pure? How should we respond to the Bible's teaching on sexual immorality?

[Discover what else Paul says about sanctification in Romans 15:16, 1 Corinthians 1:2, 1 Corinthians 6:11, 1 Corinthians 7:14, and 2 Thessalonians 2:13.]

DAY 24: SPIRIT, SOUL, AND BODY
1 THESSALONIANS 5

May your whole spirit, soul and body be kept blameless at the coming of our Lord Jesus Christ. (1 Thessalonians 5:23)

We live in the physical world. We interact with it through our senses, which allow us to see it, hear it, smell it, taste it, and touch it. It's tangible, and it's real. Contrast this with the spiritual sphere. It's not tangible, but it's nonetheless real.

We simultaneously exist in both the physical and the spiritual realms. While this is true, there's much more to it. There is a spiritual reality that is even more real than the physical realm we call home.

Consider that God exists in the spiritual realm.

It existed first and always has. It's from this spiritual reality that he created our physical world in which we live. (Don't get distracted by the details of how and when creation occurred. That's a different discussion.)

In his letter's conclusion, Paul mentions our spirit, soul, and body.

This suggests that our being—our entity—comprises spirit, soul, and body. That's something to contemplate. At first glance, we might want to reverse the order, from the most tangible to the most ethereal. We first address the body, then the soul, and the spirit last.

However, considering that God—who is spirit—made us in his image, it's appropriate to list spirit first, making it foremost. It's in our spirit—not in our body—where our primary essence subsists.

How do these three aspects of who we are interact and co-exist?

To best understand this, let's consider that we are a spirit, we have a soul, and we live in a body. This puts things in the proper order, giving us a good perspective on our existence and what's most important.

Our body—where our spirit currently lives—is temporary. It is finite and will one day die.

Our soul connects our body and our spirit. Let's view our soul as comprising our mind, will, and emotions.

Unlike our body, our spirit faces no worldly restrictions. It lives forever. That's an amazing thought to contemplate.

Although our bodies are temporal and will die, our spirits will live on, lasting for the rest of eternity in the spiritual realm.

Though it is good and right to take care of our bodies, it's wiser and better to care for our spirits. After all, we are spirits; we just live in a body.

What can we do to take better care of our bodies? What can we do to take better care of our souls? And what can we do to take better care of our spirits?

[Discover more about our body, soul, and spirit in Matthew 6:25, Luke 10:27, Galatians 6:18, and James 2:26.]

BONUS CONTENT: A HOLY KISS

Greet all God's people with a holy kiss. (1 Thessalonians 5:26)

Many churches have a time of greeting in their services. This can range from awkward to invigorating.

At some of these churches, people may offer a handshake and mumble a rote greeting. Folks in other congregations make eye contact and smile as they greet one another. And occasionally a meaningful connection begins.

At one church my wife and I visited, the minister told us to "greet one another with a holy kiss." It was creepy, marking one of my most uncomfortable church experiences. Fortunately, few people attended that Sunday, so the number of holy kisses we received was minimal.

This is biblical, with Paul mentioning it four times (1 Thessalonians 5:26, Romans 16:16, 1 Corinthians 16:20, and 2 Corinthians 13:12). But even after experiencing it, I can't describe it in any way except disturbing. And Paul doesn't explain it or offer instructions; he just says to do it.

Though we normally think of a kiss as on the lips, the ancient method was likely different. Perhaps it was lips kissing a cheek or two cheeks touching. Since neither of these is common in many cultures today, we might consider modern-day equivalents to be a hearty handshake, a pat on the back, or a meaningful fist bump. But let's not kiss unrelated people at church on the lips.

Even so, we can infer a few things about a holy kiss from what little Scripture shares.

Each time Paul mentions a holy kiss, it's in a letter to a church, so it must be just for the church community. I take this to imply that outsiders (or, in our case, church visitors) are exempt.

A kiss is an intimate sign of affection. Since the context is church, we can dismiss a holy kiss as being an act of physical intimacy, instead understanding it as spiritual intimacy.

Last, it is holy, which is something sacred; it is hallowed.

This implies that a holy kiss is a sacred act of spiritual intimacy for a church community, but I'm still not sure how to do it.

How can we best respond to this command today? How should we greet one another at our church gatherings?

[Discover more about kissing in Genesis 50:1, Exodus 4:27, Proverbs 24:26, Proverbs 27:6, Mark 14:44–46, Luke 7:38, Luke 15:20, and Acts 20:36–38. Read what Peter has to say about greeting others in 1 Peter 5:14.]

2 THESSALONIANS

The book of 2 Thessalonians is the apostle Paul's second epistle to the church in the city of Thessalonica. As with 1 Thessalonians, the letter comes from Paul, Silas, and Timothy.

In contrast to the first letter to the church in Thessalonica, which was affectionate, this epistle takes a more formal, authoritative tone. It's theological, containing teaching about the return of Jesus.

Though Paul encourages the Thessalonian church in this letter, he also scolds them for not living and acting as befitting of followers of Jesus, including the need to guard against false teaching or heresy.

DAY 25: BRING TO FRUITION
2 THESSALONIANS 1

With this in mind, we constantly pray for you, that our God may make you worthy of his calling, and that by his power he may bring to fruition your every desire for goodness and your every deed prompted by faith. (2 Thessalonians 1:11)

Paul has a two-part prayer for his friends in Thessalonica. This isn't a onetime request, but an ongoing effort. He says he prays for them continuously.

The first part of Paul's prayer is that God will make them worthy of his calling. Being worthy is a recurring theme in Paul's letters. We covered it in Day 10 for the church in Ephesus and Day 17 for the church in Colossae. Paul also addresses it in Philippians 1:27 and 1 Thessalonians 2:11–12. He repeats the idea again in his second letter to the Thessalonians.

The next element of Paul's recurring prayer for the Thessalonians is that by God's power he will bring to fruition—that is, bring about—their every desire for goodness and their every deed prompted by faith.

When most people think of desire, they view it as longing for what is wrong and not what is good. Because of sin in our world, people want selfish things. They too often crave what is evil. Many of the dictionary definitions of *desire* support this negative leaning, focusing on sexual passion.

Yet in a general sense, *desire* is to wish for or long for anything. This can be something good or something not so good.

Paul wants the Thessalonians to desire goodness. He prays that God will bring it about. God's part is to make it happen. Our part is to desire what is good. If we don't yearn for goodness, there's nothing for God to bring to fruition.

Proverbs says that the desire of the righteous ends in what is good. In contrast, what the wicked hope for produces wrath (Proverbs 11:23). If we don't see goodness surrounding us, it might be because we're not desiring it.

The other item Paul prays for is that God will bring to fruition every deed prompted by faith.

Unlike *desire*, which usually carries negative implications, *deed* normally conveys the positive. That is, most deeds are good deeds.

Given this, we can understand Paul's prayer to request that God will bring into fruition every *good* deed prompted by faith (James 2:14).

Note that this is not *every* good deed. It's every good deed prompted by faith.

This suggests that we can do good deeds for the wrong reasons. We may perform acts of goodness to elevate ourselves or get people's attention, earning their praise or admiration. This is not what Paul prays for.

As we consider Paul's prayer to the Thessalonian church, let us desire goodness and perform faith-filled good deeds. May God bring these to fruition.

What do we desire? When we do good is it prompted by faith or self-interest? Should we join Paul's prayer that God will bring goodness and good deeds to fruition in our lives?

[Discover more about deeds in Ecclesiastes 12:14, Matthew 5:16, and James 3:13.]

DAY 26: STAND FIRM
2 THESSALONIANS 2

So then, brothers and sisters, stand firm and hold fast to the teachings we passed on to you, whether by word of mouth or by letter. (2 Thessalonians 2:15)

In Day 18, we talked about the word *therefore*, which connects the prior text to what follows it. The first passage gives vital context to better inform what comes next. We should view the phrase *so then* to mean the same thing.

Paul uses *so then* often, appearing in seven of his letters and occurring seventeen times. No other Bible writer uses this phrase as much.

What's the passage that precedes *so then*?

In the prior verses, Paul talks about thanking

God for the Thessalonians. God chose them as first-fruits, saved by the Holy Spirit's sanctifying work through their belief in God's truth. He called them through the good news of Jesus. In this way, they can share in his glory.

So then—that is, because God chose, saved, and called the Thessalonian church—Paul encourages them to stand firm and hold fast to what Paul and his friends taught them.

Do stand firm and hold fast mean the same thing? Are they two phrases that communicate the same idea?

Yes, and no. Let's explore each one.

To stand firm means to be immovable. Think of being buffeted by the waves of life, yet standing firm amid the turbulence (Ephesians 4:14).

Or consider Jesus's parable of the wise and foolish builders (Luke 6:47–49). We're like a person building a house. When we hear Jesus and obey him, we dig deep to set our life's foundation on rock. We build our house (our life) upon that rock. When the waters rise and the storm strikes, the house stands firm. Our life can likewise weather the trials and storms that come our way, because it's built well on the sound foundation of Jesus.

The opposite are people who hear Jesus's words

and ignore what he says. Their life has no foundation. It will collapse in destruction when they face difficult times.

Second is to hold fast. We hold fast to Paul's teachings. It's something we cling to. When the world tries to pull us away, we tightly grip the Word of God. We hang on as if our life depends on it—because it does.

Besides clinging to what we're taught—through both our teachers and the Bible—we can cling to our Lord (Psalm 63:8) and we can cling to what is good (Romans 12:9).

As we move through life, let us stand firm on our faith foundation in Jesus, and let us cling to the truth we've learned about him.

What have we built our house (our life) on? What do we hold fast to? Have we made Jesus a priority in our lives?

[Discover more about *hold fast* in Deuteronomy 13:4, Joshua 22:5, Psalm 119:31, and Revelation 12:17.]

DAY 27: AVOID IDLENESS
2 THESSALONIANS 3

We command you, brothers and sisters, to keep away from every believer who is idle and disruptive and does not live according to the teaching you received from us. (2 Thessalonians 3:6)

Paul gives a command to the Thessalonian Church, and we can receive it as a command for us today as well. He tells them to keep away from other believers who exhibit three specific traits.

The first one is believers who are idle. The second is believers who are disruptive. And the third is believers who don't live according to what Paul and his team taught them.

Keeping away from others sounds a lot like ostracism or even shunning. We must be extremely careful in how we apply this. Most notably is that it specifically refers to other believers and doesn't apply to non-believers.

The goal of keeping away from these people isn't to punish them but to bring about their repentance of wrongdoing and restore them into the community.

Idle: When Paul was with the Thessalonian church, he gave them an example of working to supply his needs. He didn't expect handouts. He wants them to adopt the same perspective. They should work for the food they eat and not expect someone else to feed them. If they refuse to do that, they don't deserve to eat, and the other believers should keep away from them.

Disruptive: Next, we're to keep away from other believers who cause confusion or produce disorder. This doesn't mean there should be no disagreements. People will have differences of opinion. But issues shouldn't become disruptive to the functioning of the church. The brothers and sisters should stay away from other believers who cause trouble.

Sadly, Paul has heard that some of the Thessalonians are idle and disruptive.

Doesn't Live According to Paul's Teaching: Paul and the other missionaries taught the Thessalonians about Jesus and how to live out their faith in a God-honoring way. Implicitly, some of them are not doing this. Paul warns the rest of the flock to keep away from them. If they don't, there's a danger they could follow the poor example of the dissidents.

This command includes all who disregard Paul's letter. The churches are to keep away from them as well.

The purpose of withdrawing from believers who do these three things is so that they'll feel ashamed of their wrong behavior. When doing so, the church isn't to treat them as the enemy or dismiss them forever (2 Corinthians 2:6–8). The intent is to warn them as fellow believers in Christ.

Though Paul's command is to not associate with such people, the implicit encouragement is to make sure that we don't give in to any of these three issues ourselves. We are to work and not be idle. We are to build up and not disrupt. And we are to follow Paul's teaching—which aligns with God's—and not disobey it.

Are we known for being hard workers or for our idleness? When have we been busybodies? Do our lives align with what we read in Scripture?

[Discover more about idleness in Proverbs 31:27, Ecclesiastes 10:18, and 1 Thessalonians 5:14. Read what Paul says about busybodies in 1 Timothy 5:13.]

1 TIMOTHY

At this point in our study, we move from Paul's letters to churches to Paul's letters to individuals. First up are Paul's two letters to his protégé Timothy. From the tone of his writing, it's clear Paul has a deep affection for Timothy, just like a proud father to his son who faithfully follows Jesus.

When Paul traveled to Lystra, he met Timothy, who lived there. The believers in the area thought highly of the young man. Paul invited Timothy to join him on his missionary journey. Before they left, Paul circumcised Timothy (Acts 16:1–3).

Timothy's mother was Jewish and believed in Jesus. Her name was Eunice. Timothy's grandmother was Lois and also a believer (2 Timothy

1:5). Together they provided Timothy with a strong faith foundation. Timothy's father, however, was Greek.

In addition, Paul lists Timothy as a co-sender of five letters (Philippians 1:1, Colossians 1:1, 1 Thessalonians 1:1, 2 Thessalonians 1:1, and Philemon 1:1).

Paul left Timothy in Ephesus to help the church there (1 Timothy 1:3). First Timothy is a letter to this young pastor.

The books of 1 Timothy, 2 Timothy, and Titus are often called Paul's pastoral letters because their focus is on instructing young ministers. As such, many consider these three books as church manuals, more than personal letters, providing instruction that is both practical and unifying to church leaders and ministers.

However, since all followers of Jesus are called to minister to others, these three books apply to church members as well.

DAY 28: THE LAW IS GOOD
1 TIMOTHY 1

We know that the law is good if one uses it properly.
(1 Timothy 1:8)

Paul talks a lot about the law in his letters, particularly in his epistle to the Galatians (as well as Romans). It seems Paul is often critical of the law, stating that it can't save us—that only faith in Jesus can. So it may surprise us when Paul states in his letter to Timothy that the law is good.

Has Paul changed his mind about the law? No, not at all. Paul's just looking at the law from a different perspective. Remember that his other letters are to churches. To them, he must emphasize that the law can't save them, that only Jesus can.

Yet 1 Timothy is Paul's letter to a minister. Paul doesn't need to remind Timothy that salvation isn't available through the law, that it's only through faith in Jesus. Therefore, Paul wants to give Timothy a deeper understanding of the law's intended purpose. This will help the young pastor better minister to the people in the church in Ephesus.

First up, Paul clarifies that the law is good only when it's used properly. An improper use of the law is as a path to earn our salvation. We can't do that. We'll always fall short.

The law isn't for the righteous—that is, those already made right through Jesus. Instead, it's for everyone else. It's for those who need Jesus to save them.

Paul gives a lengthy list of who this entails. It's for lawbreakers and rebels. It's for the ungodly and the sinful. And it's for the unholy and the irreligious. The law applies to people who kill their parents, to murderers, and to the sexually immoral—specifically practicing homosexuals. The law is also for slave traders, liars, and perjurers.

This is quite a comprehensive inventory, ranging from the rare sin of murder to the more common sin of lying. Though most people have not committed many of the items on this list, it's likely we've all lied at some point.

The purpose of the law is to show people how far short they fall in meeting God's expectations. It shows people their sin.

Though sin was in the world before God gave Moses his law, people weren't held accountable for their sins because there was no law to point out their guilt (Romans 5:13).

Abraham, who lived prior to the law, believed in God. Therefore, the Lord credited righteousness to him (James 2:23). He lived by faith (Hebrews 11:8–10). So should we.

That's the purpose of the law, to point out our shortcomings and reveal that we'll never measure up on our own. Jesus is the solution. All we need to do is believe in him.

Have we ever thought that the law is good? If we've turned to Jesus to save us, how might we still be living according to the law? Is it good for us to do so?

[Discover more about salvation through Jesus in Romans 10:9.]

DAY 29: PRAY
1 TIMOTHY 2

Therefore I want the men everywhere to pray, lifting up holy hands without anger or disputing. (1 Timothy 2:8)

Paul tells Timothy that he wants men everywhere to pray, lifting holy hands without anger or disputing. The implication is that Timothy is supposed to teach this to the men in the church of Ephesus.

There's a lot in this. Let's unpack it.

First, it's to men everywhere. This implies everyone. We are to pray.

When we pray, we lift our hands. Raising our arms in prayer is a physical act of worship. It's not merely spiritual. There's a physical element as well. When we lift our hands in prayer, it's a visual encouragement to others to follow our example.

Yet these hands must be holy. The opposite of holy is unholy. Unholy hands might mean unconsecrated or ungodly. It could even mean outrageous, as in disgraceful or scandalous. Though Paul doesn't mention it in this passage, if our hands fall into any of these categories, the first step is repentance. Then we are prepared to move forward in prayer.

Next, we pray without anger. Have we ever prayed angry prayers? This might include asking God to punish people who have slighted us, hurt us, or disappointed us. God doesn't want us to pray angry prayers of retribution.

Last, we should pray without disputing, which means expressing disagreement about something or with someone. It implies struggle. We shouldn't be embroiled in conflict when we pray (Matthew 5:23–24). Some versions of the Bible render this word as *doubting* or *argument*. We should pray without doubting and free from argument.

Paul addresses his teaching to men. Does this mean it doesn't apply to women? Does this mean that women aren't supposed to pray? I doubt that's Paul's intention. Maybe Paul feels men are more in need of this instruction about prayer. This doesn't mean that women don't also need to lift holy hands in prayer without anger or disputing, but maybe this isn't as much of an issue for women.

In the verse that follows this one, Paul directs his teaching to women (1 Timothy 2:9). He tells them to dress modestly. This means decently and appropriately. They shouldn't focus on hairstyles, jewelry, or expensive clothes. Instead, they should adorn themselves with good deeds.

Does this mean men don't have to dress modestly? Does it suggest men can wear whatever they want? I likewise doubt this was Paul's intent. Similarly, maybe he recognizes that an excessive focus on personal appearance can be more of an issue for women than for men.

Regardless of our gender, men and women can likewise glean truth and encouragement from both of these verses.

What do we think about Paul directing one verse to men and the other verse to women? How can we use 1 Timothy 2:8 to better inform how we pray? How can we use 1 Timothy 2:9 to guide us in our personal appearance?

[Discover more about men and women in Genesis 1:27 and Galatians 3:28.]

DAY 30: OVERSEERS
1 TIMOTHY 3

Here is a trustworthy saying: Whoever aspires to be an overseer desires a noble task. (1 Timothy 3:1)

Paul affirms people who want to be overseers. Interestingly, he's the only New Testament writer who uses the word *overseer*.

What is an overseer? It's not a label we often hear in the church today. In a general sense, an overseer is someone who watches over the work of laborers—that is, they literally *see over* the work of others. They're like a supervisor or superintendent.

For Jesus's church, an overseer is someone who

watches over the people in the church. Paul calls this a noble task.

As Paul lists the qualifications of an overseer, he uses male pronouns and says that the overseer must be faithful to his wife. This suggests that only men can be overseers.

A few verses prior to this, Paul says that he only allows men to teach (1 Timothy 2:12). He doesn't give this as a command; it's his preference. Yet his personal perspective may skew his view of women in ministry.

Some churches take this passage in 1 Timothy to mean that only men can be overseers. Other churches remove any gender restrictions. Which is it?

What about a woman who is more qualified than a man? What if men aren't willing to become overseers and women are? These are weighty questions without a simple answer.

For more insight, let's look at some examples in the Bible of women in leadership roles.

Deborah was an Old Testament prophetess. When Barak refused to leave the army—as God commanded—Deborah stepped in (Judges 4). Other prophetesses are Huldah (2 Kings 22:14) and Isaiah's wife (Isaiah 8:3).

Moses's sister, Miriam, was a prophetess too. She also led the people in worship (Exodus 15:20–21).

In the New Testament, Jesus gives Mary Magdalene the all-important task of telling the other disciples the good news of his resurrection (John 20:17–18). This makes her the first missionary.

Phoebe is a deacon of the church in Cenchreae (Romans 16:1).

Mary, the mother of John Mark, opens her home for people to gather and pray (Acts 12:12). This is the Bible's first mention of a house church.

Priscilla and Aquila also have a house church (Romans 16:3–5). Why does Paul list Priscilla's name first and not her husband? It's likely because she takes the lead in their church.

Nympha likewise has a church that meets in her home (Colossians 4:15). Is she single? Perhaps she's married, but her husband isn't interested in meeting with Jesus's followers. Or maybe she's just a better leader.

Later, Paul talks about the qualifications for deacons. In one verse he gives the requisite traits for women (1 Timothy 3:11). This could refer to deacon's wives or to women who are deacons. It's another thing for us to ponder.

The role of women in ministry is a contentious issue. It's difficult to resolve, but consider these verses to determine how best to move forward.

How should we view people who hold a different opinion than ours about women in ministry? How have women helped us grow in our faith and become more like Jesus?

[Discover another notable woman in 2 John 1:1–6. Reread the verses about men and women in Genesis 1:27 and Galatians 3:28, from Day 29.]

DAY 31: GODLINESS
1 TIMOTHY 4

For physical training is of some value, but godliness has value for all things, holding promise for both the present life and the life to come. (1 Timothy 4:8)

Too many people in our world today don't get enough exercise. Their eating habits aren't good. They ingest too much of what they shouldn't and not enough of what they should. Their physical condition isn't good. In short, they're out of shape.

When confronted with this reality, the response of some is to exercise. They want to lose unwanted pounds and tone their physique.

Some make New Year's resolutions to exercise

or lose weight, but most soon forget their pledge and fall back into their sedentary lifestyle. But others turn their resolution into a habit. With consistent effort, their body gradually embarks on a metamorphosis, bringing about meaningful change. They get in shape; they become healthy.

Other people undergo physical activity for a particular sport or to prepare for a physically demanding endeavor. They exercise, guard what they eat, and train with intention. They have a goal in mind, and they'll do whatever it takes to reach it.

These forms of physical training have some value. Paul says so. When done properly, our bodies benefit. From that perspective, physical training will help us live longer and better lives. Given that our bodies are temples of the Holy Spirit (1 Corinthians 6:19), this is a good outcome and worthy of our attention. Yet it's not the ideal pursuit.

Better than physical training is the quest for godliness. It yields more value; it carries greater impact. Godliness provides benefits for our lives here on earth and for our future lives in heaven.

What is godliness?

Godliness is living a life aligned with God. It shows reverence, devotion, and obedience to him. It changes how we live our lives. We begin to view and treat others the way God does. We show God's love to them.

Godliness is another New Testament word, used mostly by Paul and primarily in his letters to Timothy. We're left to wonder if Paul thinks Timothy needs to do better at pursuing personal godliness or if Paul wants Timothy to encourage the church in Ephesus to do so. Perhaps it's both.

We must pursue godliness. It doesn't come naturally to most people. Just as with physical training, we must train for godliness. It takes effort, commitment, and time. Yet do we spend as much time pursuing godliness as we do with physical training?

If we exercise and care for our bodies, well done.

Yet it's even better to pursue godliness. This addresses our whole being of body, soul, and spirit. The payoff benefits us both now and forever.

How much time do we spend focusing on the condition of our physical bodies? How does this compare to the time we spend focusing on our spiritual well-being?

[Discover more about godliness in 2 Peter 1:5–7.]

DAY 32: INSTRUCTIONS FOR ELDERS
1 TIMOTHY 5

The elders who direct the affairs of the church well are worthy of double honor, especially those whose work is preaching and teaching. (1 Timothy 5:17)

Paul's use of the word *elders* in this verse seems to indicate a different office than *overseer,* which we covered in Day 30. From this verse we see that elders are those who handle the activities of the church. Two key activities are preaching and teaching.

Preaching and teaching seem like synonyms. Yet in Scripture preaching is often directed to those on the outside—to people who need to hear Jesus's good news. In contrast, teaching often addresses those on the inside—to those who already follow Jesus.

These elders are worthy of double honor. We might consider *double honor* to mean well paid or highly appreciated. Likely both.

Regarding compensation, Paul backs up his teaching with two verses from Scripture. First is not to prohibit an ox from eating while it treads out the grain (Deuteronomy 25:4). The other passage comes from Jesus himself when he says that the worker deserves his wages (Luke 10:7). The context refers to food and lodging.

We contrast this teaching from Paul with his own practice of sometimes working to pay his own way and not depend on others (Acts 18:1–3, 1 Thessalonians 2:9, and 1 Corinthians 4:12). Paul's decision to pay his own way, however, was a choice he made and not one that was forced upon him (2 Corinthians 11:7). It's not a command for others to obey, though they may likewise opt to follow his example.

Yet other times Paul receives financial support (2 Corinthians 11:8–9).

When it comes to financially compensating our

elders who preach and teach, we should be careful to avoid extremes. Paying them too little shows disrespect and isn't God-honoring. Yet paying too much could unwisely elevate them and unnecessarily overburden givers.

We must also include the ideas of appreciation and respect in this discussion. Our elders deserve that too.

We should also be careful what we say about our church elders. We must avoid unnecessary criticism. Instead, we should honor them for the important role they play in our spiritual community and growth.

Though Paul's teaching specifically addresses elders, we may wonder if it applies to today's ministers. Most ministers also manage the church's activities, preach, and teach. They deserve a double honor as well. This includes their financial compensation and our verbal support for what they do.

How well do we do at giving our elders and our ministers a double honor? How do we view the compensation of our church staff? When have we given unwarranted criticism to those elders who preach and teach?

[Discover more about honor to leaders in Acts 5:34 and Acts 28:10. Read more about this topic in Luke 20:46 and James 3:1.]

DAY 33: GREAT GAIN
1 TIMOTHY 6

But godliness with contentment is great gain. (1 Timothy 6:6)

In today's passage, Paul warns Timothy to watch out for false teachers. False teachers are conceited and lack understanding. They fixate on controversy and argue about the meaning of words (2 Timothy 2:14 and 2 Timothy 2:23). In doing so, they produce much conflict. Paul concludes his warning with the announcement that they think godliness is a way to make money.

This is the backdrop for today's focus verse. In view of those who think godliness is a means for financial gain, Paul says that godliness *with* contentment is great gain. That is, pairing godliness with contentment produces an even greater outcome.

We talked about godliness in Day 31. There we said that godliness is living a life aligned with God, showing reverence, devotion, and obedience to him. It views and treats others the way God does. It shows God's love.

When false teachers put on an air of godliness, they don't do it for God or for the people. They do so to enrich themselves financially. They're greedy.

Paul doesn't criticize them for their behavior as much as he criticizes them for their motivation. They want money; they want more.

It's in response to this that Paul links contentment with godliness. Pursuing them in tandem is the way to great gain.

When Paul says *great gain*, however, he doesn't likely refer to the financial gain that the false teachers seek. Instead, he probably means an even more important result, which is spiritual gain.

Godliness is how we live our lives. Contentment is our attitude toward the life we lead.

We're wrong to view godliness as being a life of sacrifice. It's not something to suffer through but something to rejoice in. That's why we need to be content. We must seek contentment in the life we live.

To put things in perspective, Paul says that just as we brought nothing into this world when we were born, we'll take nothing from it when we die. The possessions, property, and money we strive for in this life will mean nothing to us when our life ends.

Instead, we should aim for contentment. Paul says if we have food and clothing, that should be enough (1 Timothy 6:8). This is certainly something to contemplate.

Paul has learned to be content whatever the situation (Philippians 4:11–12). We should strive to do the same. Our godliness and contentment will result in great gain.

What is our view of godliness? How well do we do at being content in every situation? What does great gain mean to us?

[Discover more about contentment in Luke 3:14 and Hebrews 13:5.]

2 TIMOTHY

The book of 2 Timothy is the apostle Paul's second letter to the younger minister Timothy. It's also the second of Paul's three pastoral letters, which focus on guiding young ministers.

Paul wrote his first letter to Timothy when the young pastor was in Ephesus. Yet it seems Timothy is somewhere else when Paul writes his second letter (2 Timothy 4:12–13).

Whereas Paul's first letter to Timothy is essentially a manual for church management, his second letter reads more like a last will and testament. It gives parting instructions to Timothy, encouraging him to persevere after Paul's death, as well as more advice on how to deal with false teaching.

DAY 34: CALLED TO HOLY LIVING
2 TIMOTHY 1

He has saved us and called us to a holy life—not because of anything we have done but because of his own purpose and grace. (2 Timothy 1:9)

Paul reminds Timothy that God has saved us, but this is not because of our efforts. We can't earn it; we don't merit it. Instead, our salvation is a result of his purpose for us and is accomplished through his grace. We covered this truth that we are saved by grace through faith in Day 8. There's nothing we can do to earn God's marvelous favor and immense love for us (Ephesians 2:8–9).

The other part of today's verse is God's call for

us to live a holy life. This is a recurring theme of Paul's. In Day 10 it was to live a life worthy. In Day 14 it was to work out our salvation. And in Day 17 it was to please our Lord. These are all variations of the same theme.

In short, we live a worthy life, work out our salvation, and please our Lord in response to what he has already done for us. We don't do these things to get his attention, garner special favor, or receive heavenly accolades. We do them out of gratitude to him, for saving us when he had no reason to—other than because he wanted to.

Now we have a fourth way of looking at the same concept. We live a holy life.

What does this mean?

Living a holy life involves changing our perspective in how we live from being self-centered to being God-focused. It's a highly moral lifestyle that we embark upon for a spiritual purpose—for God, who loves us and saves us, even though we don't deserve it.

Holy living is also saintly. This doesn't mean our life is perfect from a biblical perspective. It doesn't mean that we perfectly honor God in every way and in all that we do. Instead, saintly merely means that we're moving in that direction. Our purpose in doing so isn't to get anything. Instead, it honors our Lord for all he's done for us.

Living a holy life is very similar to living a life of righteousness. We do this by faith (Habakkuk 2:4, Romans 1:17, and Galatians 3:11).

Living a life of righteousness leads to holiness (Romans 6:19). This verse connects holy living with righteousness. God invites us to pursue both.

Do we feel God has called us to live a holy life? What are we doing as a result? What is our attitude toward our effort and the outcome it will produce?

[Discover more about living holy lives in Romans 12:1 and 1 Peter 2:5.]

DAY 35: FOUR THINGS TO PURSUE
2 TIMOTHY 2

Flee the evil desires of youth and pursue righteousness, faith, love and peace, along with those who call on the Lord out of a pure heart. (2 Timothy 2:22)

Paul gives instructions to his protégé that we should all hear—and pursue. Though Timothy is his primary audience, Paul's advice is helpful to all ministers, as well as each of us who follow Jesus.

First, Paul says to run from youthful impulses. This could be to flee from sexual desire. Given the sex-saturated culture we live in today, we all need to heed this instruction—regardless of our age.

Yet there are other youthful longings to avoid as

well. This could be making a lot of money, owning a luxurious house—or two, or living an extravagant lifestyle that others would envy.

We are to flee from these desires. We replace them with four pursuits.

The first is righteousness. The second is faith, and the third is love, followed by peace. We do these things with a pure heart along with all who call Jesus their Lord.

Righteousness is right living. It's very similar to holy living, which we covered in Day 34. From a spiritual standpoint, we are made righteous when we follow Jesus. From a physical standpoint, however, right living is something we must strive for.

Next up is faith. We take our first step of faith when we believe in Jesus to save us. Then we take additional steps of faith every day thereafter. Faith is believing that we will receive what we hope for but have not yet seen (Hebrews 11:1).

By faith Noah built a large boat when there was no logical reason to do so (Genesis 6:12–22). By faith Abram (Abraham) left home to travel to a place God would show him (Genesis 12:1). And by faith Ananias went to talk to Saul, despite the risk of arrest or death (Acts 9:1–18).

Our third pursuit is to love. The Bible talks

much about love (1 Corinthians 13:4–7). First, we are to love God with all our heart, soul, mind, and strength (Mark 12:30). Then we are to love everyone else as much as we love ourselves (Mark 12:31).

Our final pursuit is peace. Peace is a quiet calm. It's the lack of hostility and the absence of strife. We are to make every effort to do what leads to peace (Romans 14:19). God will bless us when we strive to make peace (Matthew 5:9).

Therefore, we must pursue righteousness, faith, love, and peace.

How are we doing in fleeing youthful desires? What role do righteousness, faith, love, and peace play in our lives? Do we live our lives out of a pure heart?

[Discover more about a pure heart in Psalm 24:4, Psalm 51:10, Proverbs 22:11, and 1 Timothy 1:5.]

BONUS CONTENT: ALL SCRIPTURE

All Scripture is God-breathed and is useful for teaching, rebuking, correcting and training in righteousness, so that the servant of God may be thoroughly equipped for every good work. (2 Timothy 3:16–17)

Paul writes to Timothy, reminding him that he has known the Holy Scriptures since he was a young child. This knowledge has made him wise about salvation in Jesus, through faith (2 Timothy 3:15).

Paul confirms that all parts of Scripture have value. It can teach us, rebuke us, correct us, and train us for right living. This prepares us to do good.

All Scripture means every verse—not just some

or the parts we like. It's also the passages that confuse us, confound us, and confront us.

When Paul wrote this, he was referring to the Scripture in existence at that time. This certainly included what we now call the Old Testament. It also likely included what we now call the Apocrypha.

The Apocrypha was part of the Septuagint, a Greek translation of Scripture in widespread use during Jesus's time. (The Apocrypha was also in the original King James Version but was later removed.) Jesus quoted from the Septuagint and so did the New Testament writers, including Paul.

Therefore, Paul likely had the Apocrypha in mind, along with the Old Testament, when he said that God inspired all Scripture, making it useful for educating and equipping us.

Although the New Testament didn't exist when Paul wrote this truth to Timothy, we aren't in error to expand Paul's teaching of *every Scripture* to include the New Testament books too.

May we know the Holy Scriptures—the written word of God—just like Timothy and Paul. Let us teach them to our children, beginning as soon as possible.

As we read our Bible, may we use every part of it to teach us, rebuke us, correct us, and train us.

How well do we do at letting the Bible teach, rebuke, correct, and train us? What is our understanding of all Scripture? How should we treat those who hold a different view?

[Discover more in Joshua 1:8, Proverbs 22:6, John 5:39–40, and Acts 17:11.]

DAY 36: FINISH STRONG
2 TIMOTHY 3–4

I have fought the good fight, I have finished the race, I have kept the faith. (2 Timothy 4:7)

In our introduction to Paul's second letter to Timothy, we noted it reads like a last will and testament. It also gives final instructions to Timothy, so we shouldn't be surprised with today's verse.

Paul realizes his time to depart this earth approaches (2 Timothy 4:6). Toward this end, he says he's being poured out like a drink offering. He also mentions this to the Philippian church (Philippians 2:17).

A drink offering is first described in the book of

Genesis. It's Jacob's response to his encounter with God (Genesis 35:14). Visually, once poured out, the drink offering is given irrevocably. Paul sees this happening in his own life. He's completely giving everything to tell others about Jesus.

With his approaching death in view, Paul anticipates his future. He sees a crown of righteousness awaiting him, which Jesus will award to him—and to all of us (2 Timothy 4:8).

From this perspective, Paul summarizes his life from the vantage point that he is about to die. He fought well, finished his race, and kept the faith.

As Paul wraps up his first letter to Timothy, he uses similar language, encouraging Timothy to fight the good fight of faith (1 Timothy 6:12). Now Paul affirms he did exactly what he told Timothy to do. He fought the good fight. How this must encourage Timothy, knowing that his mentor accomplished one of the things he instructed his protégé to do.

Though we may not think of our life with Jesus as being a good fight, recall that our battle isn't physical but spiritual (Ephesians 6:12). Our enemy opposes us, and we must fight against him (1 Peter 5:8). When we do, we fight the good fight.

Next, Paul confirms he finished his race. He ran well and crossed the finish line. He did what God told him to do. Paul often uses the analogy of running a race in his letters (1 Corinthians 9:24 and Galatians 5:7).

Earlier in his ministry, Paul checked with other leaders of Jesus's church to make sure he was running in the right direction, that he was not running in vain (Galatians 2:2). Affirmed that he was on the right track, Paul persevered in his race.

Last, he kept the faith—that is, his faith in Jesus. Paul writes about faith in each of his letters. He says he lives by faith (Galatians 2:20). He talks about the unity of faith (Ephesians 4:13). And he writes about a shield of faith, which protects against the enemy's flaming arrows (Ephesians 6:16 and Day 12).

Let us be like Paul and finish our race strong. How we start life doesn't matter, but how we end matters more than anything.

How are we doing at fighting the good fight? Are we on track to finish our race? Are we keeping the faith? How committed are we to finishing strong?

[Discover more about Paul's outlook on his life in Acts 20:24.]

TITUS

As with 1 and 2 Timothy, Paul wrote the book of Titus to a younger minister. His name is Titus. The book of Titus stands as Paul's third pastoral letter.

Titus ministered on the island of Crete. His initial task was to appoint elders in every town (Titus 1:5). This suggests each town on the large island had its own church or gathering. In this way, we see Titus much like a circuit minister, traveling from town to town to serve multiple congregations.

Paul's letter to Titus, a charming and affectionate epistle, is not only a personal letter to Titus but also a letter to all who minister in Jesus's church. This includes both paid clergy and the laity, for all who follow Jesus are to minister to others (Romans

15:14). Paul provides guidance and instruction for effective living as a follower of Jesus.

In reading Titus, we will see many ideas and passages that parallel 1 and 2 Timothy. These include appointing elders; opposing rebellious people and heresy; teaching sound doctrine; instructions to men, women, slaves, and masters; living godly lives; being subject to those in authority; salvation in Jesus by God's grace; and the Holy Spirit.

We should not, however, let these recurring themes dissuade us from reading Titus. Instead, we should embrace this letter for its reinforcement of key truths for ministers, leaders, and all who follow Jesus.

DAY 37: ACTIONS MATTER
TITUS 1

They claim to know God, but by their actions they deny him.
(Titus 1:16)

In his letter to Titus, Paul quotes a Cretan philosopher who writes about his own people, calling them liars, evil brutes, and lazy gluttons. Paul agrees with his scathing assessment of the people who live on the island of Crete.

Paul tells Timothy to rebuke them—to rebuke them sharply.

These are not people who are outside of Jesus's church; these people are part of it. They claim to know God, but their actions don't back it up.

We've likely met people like them. They declare

they're Christians, but there's nothing in their lives to support their assertions. Their conduct is like everyone else in the world, maybe even worse.

Some of them may think that making a onetime decision to follow Jesus is enough. This allows them to live whatever lives they want to with no worry over the eternal consequences. Their faulty reasoning is that just as they were saved by grace, they can live unrestrained, sinful lives and showcase God's grace even more. Paul says, "No way!" (Romans 6:1–2).

Other people may think that showing up for church a couple of times a year or making an occasional small contribution will offset a life that doesn't honor God. That doesn't work either.

The lives these people lead are terrible witnesses to a world that needs to know Jesus.

James addresses this situation as well (James 2:14–26). He writes about the importance of showing our faith by what we do. He asks pointedly, if someone claims to have faith, but doesn't back it up with action, can that faith save them? Perhaps— but maybe not.

Instead, James encourages people to show their faith through their deeds—through what they do.

Then, their faith—as shown by their actions—is clear to everyone.

Merely believing in the one true God is not enough. Even the demons believe that, and the very thought makes them shudder.

James shares an unlikely pair of Old Testament characters who showed their faith in action. The first is Father Abraham, also called Abram (Genesis 15:6). The second is the prostitute Rahab (Joshua 6:22–25). Both proved their faith in God by what they did.

James concludes by saying that faith without deeds is dead. Paul agrees.

Do we claim to know God? Do our actions support our claim? If arrested for being a Christian, would there be enough evidence to convict us?

[Discover more about faith in action in Matthew 25:33–46 and John 13:35.]

DAY 38: SAY NO TO UNGODLINESS
TITUS 2

[God's grace] teaches us to say "No" to ungodliness and worldly passions, and to live self-controlled, upright and godly lives in this present age. (Titus 2:12)

Just as Paul wrote to Timothy with instructions about teaching specific things to different sets of people, Paul now shares similar thoughts with Titus. These people groups include older men, older women, younger women, and younger men. Paul also gives instructions to slaves.

Salvation through God's grace is offered to all these people. That grace teaches us to say *no* to ungodliness and worldly passions.

We talked about godliness—the opposite of ungodliness—in Days 31 and 33. There we said that godliness is living lives aligned with God, showing reverence, devotion, and obedience in how we live each day. Conversely, ungodliness means a lack of respect for God. It's sinful, wicked, and impious. God's grace teaches us to say *no* to ungodliness.

Next is passion. We talked about passions in Days 19, 23, and 25. Though our passions can be a longing for either good things or wrong things, typically our passions are worldly. These worldly passions crave what is evil and are often sexual. God's grace teaches us to say *no* to worldly passions.

In place of ungodliness and worldly passions, we are to live self-controlled, upright, and godly lives. Our actions matter, which we covered in Day 37.

In place of saying *no* to ungodliness and worldly passions, we should say *yes* to self-controlled, upright, and godly living.

When we focus on not doing certain things, this calls our attention to them, making it psychologically harder for us to push them aside. The better action is to give our attention to what we *should* do. Our focus likewise calls our attention to them, making it easier for us to make them part of our lives.

What we need to say *yes* to—what we must focus on—is exercising self-control. We should likewise concentrate on upright behavior, which is adhering to moral principles and living righteously. Third, let us give our attention to godly lifestyles, doing only what honors God.

We say *yes* to these things as we live our lives here on earth, waiting for the hope we have in what happens next through Jesus. Giving himself for us, our Savior redeemed us and purified us, making us his own people.

Mindful of this, we should be eager to do what is good.

Do we focus on what we should do or what we shouldn't do? What do we think about Jesus redeeming and purifying us? What do we think about us being his own people?

[Discover more about ungodliness in Isaiah 32:6, Jeremiah 23:15, and Jude 1:15.]

DAY 39: A TRUSTWORTHY SAYING
TITUS 3

This is a trustworthy saying. (Titus 3:8)

Paul gives Timothy a trustworthy saying. Though he states his intent clearly, we need to search a bit to discover precisely what this trustworthy saying is. It's not the text that follows it, so it must be the words that precede it.

Paul establishes the foundation for his trustworthy saying beginning with verse three, building up to a conclusion which starts in the middle of verse five.

Paul writes, "He saved us through the washing of rebirth and renewal by the Holy Spirit, whom he poured out on us generously through Jesus Christ our Savior, so that, having been justified by his grace, we might become heirs having the hope of eternal life" (Titus 3:5–7).

This is Paul's trustworthy saying. It's not a pithy one-liner that we can say with ease, so we must examine his words carefully.

Given the context, *he* refers to Father God, who sent us the Holy Spirit through Jesus Christ. This confirms that all three parts of the Trinity are involved in our salvation. Though Jesus's sacrificial death in our place for all our sins is the essential element of our redemption, our Heavenly Father was behind it, and the Holy Spirit amplifies it.

Our salvation washes us clean from our sins when we are born again—by our rebirth through Jesus. The Holy Spirit—sent to us by Father God through Jesus—then renews us. As a result, we are justified; that is, we're made right by his grace. Grace is receiving good things that we don't deserve.

We pair God's grace with his mercy. Mercy is not getting the punishment we deserve.

Our salvation through Jesus is an act of God's grace and his mercy. It's not something we receive through our right behavior. We read this truth in the sentence just before Paul's trustworthy saying (Titus 3:4–5).

Paul urges Titus to stress this truth to everyone who trusts in God to save them. *Everyone* includes us today. Our right response to God's gift of salvation is to dedicate ourselves to doing what is good and honorable. This benefits everyone.

What do we think about the Father, Son, and Holy Spirit all having a role in our salvation? What can we do to embrace God's mercy and grace? How well have we done at devoting ourselves to doing what is good?

[Discover the other four times Paul gives trustworthy sayings in 1 Timothy 1:15, 1 Timothy 3:1, 1 Timothy 4:9, and 2 Timothy 2:11.]

BONUS CONTENT: PAUL REFERENCES THE OLD TESTAMENT

I have hidden your word in my heart that I might not sin against you. (Psalm 119:11)

Some of Paul's letters include Old Testament references, with Galatians leading all ten epistles that we've covered in this book. Paul knows the Scriptures well—he has hidden them in his heart—and he often includes them in his letters.

Here are the seventeen verses in these letters of Paul that connect with the Old Testament.

- Galatians 3:6 quotes Genesis 15:6
- Galatians 3:8 references Genesis 12:3, 18:18, and 22:18
- Galatians 3:10 cites Deuteronomy 27:26
- Galatians 3:11 cites Habakkuk 2:4
- Galatians 3:12 cites Leviticus 18:5
- Galatians 3:13 cites Deuteronomy 21:23
- Galatians 3:16 references Genesis 12:7, 13:15, and 24:7
- Galatians 4:27 cites Isaiah 54:1
- Galatians 4:30 cites Genesis 21:10
- Galatians 5:14 quotes Leviticus 19:18

- Ephesians 4:8 cites Psalm 68:18
- Ephesians 4:26 draws from Psalm 4:4
- Ephesians 5:31 quotes Genesis 2:24
- Ephesians 6:3 cites Deuteronomy 5:16

- Philippians 2:15 cites Deuteronomy 32:5

- 1 Timothy 5:18 quotes Deuteronomy 25:4
- 1 Timothy 5:18 also quotes Luke 10:7

How well do we know Scripture? How many verses can we quote?

[Discover more about studying Scripture in Ezra 7:10 and John 5:39–40.]

PHILEMON

Paul wrote a letter to Philemon and the church that met in his home.

On the surface, Paul's epistle seems like personal correspondence, and its inclusion in the Bible is perplexing. Given that it's also addressed to the church that meets in Philemon's house, however, it's clear that Paul intended it as more than a private communication.

The book of Philemon addresses doing what is right in God's eyes and forgoing personal rights and what would be acceptable action from a legal or societal standpoint. This example has wide-reaching applications for us today.

DAY 40: PRAYER
PHILEMON 1

I always thank my God as I remember you in my prayers.
(Philemon 1:4)

If you read it quickly, Paul's letter to Philemon seems trivial and there's little to glean from it. On the surface, it's a personal request from Paul to Philemon about his slave Onesimus.

Onesimus ran away from Philemon, met Paul, and learned about Jesus. Paul's letter seeks to restore Onesimus into a right relationship with Philemon and to get approval from his master for Onesimus to help Paul.

Paul writes persuasively, using powerful

language to accomplish his goal. By the end of the letter, we expect Philemon to do as Paul requested.

Given this as the letter's purpose, it's easy to rush past a few verses in the beginning. There Paul says he always thanks God as he remembers Philemon in his prayers. Though this might seem like an inflated claim to flatter Philemon, this isn't likely the case.

Prayer is a recurring theme in Paul's letters, occurring in all of them except for Galatians and Titus. When we include Romans and 1 and 2 Corinthians, Paul mentions prayer fifty times in his letters.

This shows us just how important prayer is to him. It should likewise be important to us. But is it?

In many of his epistles, Paul tells the recipients that he thanks God for them when he thinks about them and in his prayers (Ephesians 1:16, Philippians 1:3, Colossians 1:3, 1 Thessalonians 1:2, 2 Thessalonians 1:3, 2 Timothy 1:3, and Philemon 1:4).

Paul says he *always* thanks God for them. Not occasionally, not some of the time, but always. No other biblical writer makes this claim.

Most of Paul's mentions of prayer reflect this attitude of thanksgiving. Many other verses reveal his prayer practices. Sometimes he requests that people pray for him. Interestingly, he gives instructions about prayer only three times (Colossians 4:2, 1 Thessalonians 5:17, and 1 Timothy 2:8). But mostly when Paul talks about prayer, it's in thankfulness to God for the people he's writing to.

In this way, Paul models prayer for us. We can learn much from him about his prayer practices, especially in thanking our Lord for his work in the lives of other people.

Though I often pray for others and strive to thank God for answered prayers, I seldom consider thanking God for these people.

Yet in reading about Paul and his example, I'm reminded that I need to thank God for other people who are part of Jesus's church, for how he's at work in the lives they lead, and for the way their faith encourages me and others.

How might we want to change our prayer practices to align with Paul's example? What else can we learn from Paul about prayer? Who might we want to thank God for?

[Discover other things we can always do in Psalm 16:8, Psalm 71:14, Luke 21:36, Acts 24:16, and 1 Peter 3:15.]

If you liked *Paul's Short Letters Bible Study*, please leave a review online. Your review will help others discover this book and encourage them to read it too.

Thank you.

BOOKS IN THE 40-DAY
BIBLE STUDY SERIES

Which book do you want to read next in the 40-Day Bible Study Series?

Dear Theophilus (the Gospel of Luke)

Acts Bible Study

Isaiah Bible Study

Minor Prophets Bible Study

Job Bible Study

Living Water (John)

Love Is Patient (1 and 2 Corinthians)

Revelation Bible Study

1, 2, & 3 John Bible Study

Hebrews Bible Study

James and Jude Bible Study

Matthew Bible Study

1 & 2 Peter Bible Study

Mark Bible Study

Romans Bible Study

FOR SMALL GROUPS, SUNDAY SCHOOL, AND CLASSES

Paul's Short Letters Bible Study makes an ideal eight-week Bible study discussion guide for small groups, Sunday School, and classes. To prepare for the conversation, read one chapter of this book each weekday, Monday through Friday.

- Week 1: read Days 1 through 5.
- Week 2: read Days 6 through 10.
- Week 3: read Days 11 through 15.
- Week 4: read Days 16 through 20.
- Week 5: read Days 21 through 25.
- Week 6: read Days 26 through 30.
- Week 7: read Days 31 through 35.
- Week 8: read Days 36 through 40.

When you get together, discuss the questions at the end of each chapter. The leader can use all the questions to guide your discussion or pick which ones to focus on.

Before you begin, pray as a group. Ask for Holy Spirit insight and clarity.

As you consider each chapter's questions:

- Look for how this can grow your understanding of the Bible.
- Evaluate how this can expand your faith perspective.
- Consider what you need to change in how you live your lives.

End by asking God to help apply what you've learned.

May God bless you as you read and study his Word.

IF YOU'RE NEW TO THE BIBLE

Each entry in this book contains Bible references. These can guide you if you want to learn more. If you're not familiar with the Bible, here's an overview to get you started, give some context, and minimize confusion.

First, the Bible is a collection of works written by various authors over several centuries. Think of the Bible as a diverse anthology of godly communication. It contains historical accounts, poetry, songs, letters of instruction and encouragement, messages from God sent through his representatives, and prophecies.

Most versions of the Bible have sixty-six books grouped into two sections: The Old Testament and the New Testament. The Old Testament contains thirty-nine books that precede and anticipate Jesus. The New Testament includes twenty-seven books and covers Jesus's life and the work of his followers.

The reference notations in the Bible, such as Romans 3:23, are analogous to line numbers in a Shakespearean play. They serve as a study aid. Since the Bible is much longer and more complex than a play, its reference notations are more involved.

As already mentioned, the Bible is an amalgam of books, or sections, such as Genesis, Psalms, or Matthew. These are the names given to them, over time, based on the piece's author, audience, or purpose.

In the 1200s, each book was divided into chapters, such as Acts 2 or Psalm 23. In the 1500s, the chapters were further subdivided into verses, such as John 3:16. Let's use this as an example.

The name of the book (John) appears first, followed by the chapter number (3), a colon, and then the verse number (16). Sometimes called a chapter-verse reference notation, this helps people quickly find a specific text regardless of their version of the Bible.

Although the goal was to place these chapter and verse divisions at logical breaks, they sometimes seem arbitrary. Therefore, it's good practice to read what precedes and follows each passage you're studying. The text before or after it may contain relevant insights into the portion you're exploring.

Here's how to look up a specific passage in the Bible based on its reference: Most Bibles contain a table of contents, which gives the page number for the beginning of each book. Start there. Locate the book you want to read, and turn to that page. Then flip forward to the chapter you want. Last, skim that chapter to locate the specific verse.

If you want to read online, enter the reference into BibleGateway.com or BibleHub.com. Also check out the YouVersion Bible app.

Learn more about the greatest book ever written at ABibleADay.com, which provides a Bible blog, summaries of the books of the Bible, a dictionary of Bible terms, Bible reading plans, and other resources.

ABOUT PETER DEHAAN

Peter DeHaan, PhD, wants to change the world one word at a time. His books and blog posts discuss God, the Bible, and church, geared toward spiritual seekers and church dropouts. Many people feel church has let them down, and Peter seeks to encourage them as they search for a place to belong.

But he's not afraid to ask tough questions or make religious people squirm. He's not trying to be provocative. Instead, he seeks truth, even if it makes people uncomfortable. Writing from a biblical worldview, Peter urges Christians to push past the status quo and reexamine how they practice their faith in every part of their lives.

Peter earned his doctorate, awarded with high distinction, from Trinity College of the Bible and Theological Seminary. He lives with his wife in beautiful Southwest Michigan and wrangles cross-word puzzles in his spare time.

A lifelong student of Scripture, Peter wrote the

1,000-page website ABibleADay.com to encourage people to explore the Bible, the greatest book ever written. His popular blog, at PeterDeHaan.com, addresses biblical Christianity to build a faith that matters.

Read his blog, receive his newsletter, and learn more at PeterDeHaan.com.

BOOKS BY PETER DEHAAN

40-DAY BIBLE STUDY SERIES

Dear Theophilus (the Gospel of Luke)

Acts Bible Study

Isaiah Bible Study

Minor Prophets Bible Study

Job Bible Study

Living Water (John)

Love Is Patient (1 and 2 Corinthians)

Revelation Bible Study

1, 2, & 3 John Bible Study

Hebrews Bible Study

James and Jude Bible Study

Matthew Bible Study

1 & 2 Peter Bible Study

Mark Bible Study

Romans Bible Study

HOLIDAY CELEBRATION DEVOTIONALS

The Advent of Jesus

The Passion of Jesus (Lent)

The Victory of Jesus (Easter)

The Ministry of Jesus

Thanksgiving with Jesus

New Year with Jesus

BIBLE CHARACTER SKETCHES SERIES

Women of the Bible

The Friends and Foes of Jesus

Old Testament Sinners and Saints

More Old Testament Sinners and Saints

Heroes and Heavies of the Apocrypha

200 Old Testament Sinners and Saints

VISITING CHURCHES SERIES

52 Churches

The 52 Churches Workbook

More Than 52 Churches

The More Than 52 Churches Workbook

Visiting Online Church

Shopping for Church

OTHER BOOKS

Elephant God

Jesus's Broken Church

Martin Luther's 95 Theses

The Christian Church's LGBTQ Failure

Bridging the Sacred-Secular Divide

Beyond Psalm 150

For the latest list of all Peter's books, go to
PeterDeHaan.com/nonfiction.